The Workbook on ABIDING IN CHRIST

THE WAY OF LIVING PRAYER

MAXIE DUNNAM

AUTHOR OF

THE WORKBOOK OF LIVING PRAYER

The Workbook on Abiding in Christ: The Way of Living Prayer

The Upper Room Web site: www.upperroom.org

Scripture quotations marked as AP indicate "author's paraphrase."

An extension of the copyright page appears on page 199.

Cover image: Anneclaire Le Royer / iStock Images
Cover design: Gore Studio, Inc. / www.gorestudio.com
Interior design: Nancy Terzian / www.buckinghorsedesign.com

Library of Congress Cataloging-in-Publication Data

Dunnam, Maxie D.
The workbook on abiding in christ : the way of living prayer / Maxie Dunnam.
p. cm.
Includes bibliographical references.
ISBN 978-0-8358-1028-9
1. Prayer—Study and teaching. 2. Spiritual life—Christianity. I. Title.
BV214.D86 2010
248.3'2—dc22

2010006585

Printed in the United States of America

Praise for *The Workbook on Abiding in Christ*

For many years Maxie Dunnam has been our reliable guide on the way to living prayer. This new workbook is a wonderful gift that guides us, step-by-step, into true abiding in Christ.

—William H. Willimon
Bishop, Birmingham Area
The United Methodist Church

The Workbook on Abiding in Christ is a practical, personal, and profound companion volume to Maxie Dunnam's classic, *The Workbook of Living Prayer*. If you want to have a deeper experience of the apostle Paul's number one teaching point—living *in* Christ by abiding in his love—this is the book to read.

—Gary W. Moon, MDiv, PhD
Vice President and Integration Chair, Richmont Graduate University
Author, *Apprenticeship with Jesus*

Maxie Dunnam's *Workbook on Abiding in Christ* is an enriching and challenging small-group resource for those seeking to grow in their faith. It is an excellent sequel to his widely used *Workbook of Living Prayer*. The author builds on the same essential disciplines of spiritual reading, engagement with scripture, personal reflection, and small-group sharing. I believe that participants will find that the simple but dynamic process outlined in this resource will lead to life-changing experiences and a new awareness of the indwelling Christ as the shaping power of daily life.

—Janice T. Grana,
Former Editor and Publisher, The Upper Room

I can remember where I was when it happened! It was one morning when Maxie Dunnam and I were riding together to The Upper Room. When we rode together, we edited each other's stuff.

Maxie said, "I've been thinking about a workbook to help people learn how to pray." I said, "That's the dumbest idea I've ever heard. People can't learn how to pray from a workbook." (That's how much I knew about workbooks and about prayer—and about Maxie.)

We worked on *The Workbook of Living Prayer* during several trips, and it was beginning to come together. As we ended a particularly insightful session, I commented, "I didn't think you would be able to do this, but it's going to work." Did it ever! It was a divine idea.

Maxie pioneered the workbook genre of spiritual formation small-group learning.

Fourteen workbooks later, he has done it again in *The Workbook on Abiding in Christ*. He presents weekly, essential biblical and theological markers about how to *abide in Christ*. Individuals and small groups are given didactic handles to our faith. All who have benefited from Maxie's previous workbooks will discover that they were necessary preludes to *abiding in Christ*.

— Danny E. Morris,
Former Director of Developing Ministries, The Upper Room

To my wife, Jerry

The love of Jesus in me greets the love of Jesus in you and brings us together in the name of the Father, and the Son, and the Holy Spirit.

For fifty-three years we have loved and shared our lives. You have not only kept our love and the love of our family alive in a self-giving, creative way; you have been a great source for my abiding in Christ. My prayer is that I have been "as good for you" as you have been for me.

Lord, give us the grace to be completely yours.

OTHER WORKBOOKS BY MAXIE DUNNAM

The Workbook of Living Prayer

The Workbook on Becoming Alive in Christ

The Workbook on the Beatitudes (with Kimberly Dunnam Reisman)

The Workbook on the Christian Walk

The Workbook of Intercessory Prayer

The Workbook on Keeping Company with the Saints

The Workbook on the Seven Deadly Sins (with Kimberly Dunnam Reisman)

The Workbook on Spiritual Disciplines

The Workbook on the Ten Commandments (with Kimberly Dunnam Reisman)

The Workbook on Virtues and the Fruit of the Spirit (with Kimberly Dunnam Reisman)

CONTENTS

INTRODUCTION

If anyone ever assesses my contribution to the church and living the Christian life, I believe they will conclude that one of my greatest contributions is *The Workbook of Living Prayer*. Originally published in 1974, the workbook has been translated into at least ten languages (we continue to discover language translations we didn't know about) and has sold over a million copies in English. Hardly a week goes by without my receiving a note or a comment from someone, sharing what this workbook has meant to that person and to entire congregations.

I believe that the workbook's uniqueness and effectiveness is not its content but its *dynamic*. We have great literature on prayer. Many outstanding Christian leaders have written on the theme. As a novice in prayer, I prayed in fear and trembling, believing that many people read scores of the greatest books on prayer, but they still do not pray. The workbook dynamic was a gift of the Spirit. It is almost impossible to use *The Workbook of Living Prayer* without praying. Brief teaching segments, engagement with scripture, the challenge of reflecting and recording (I call it "praying at the point of a pencil"), suggestions for taking the learning or experience from the prayer time into the day, and guides for group sharing—all combine to create a dynamic where prayer *happens* without deliberate intention. So, in using the workbook, you do not simply read about prayer; you will also pray.

HOW I CAME TO WRITE THIS BOOK

This book is a sequel to *The Workbook of Living Prayer*. For some time the editors at Upper Room Books have been requesting that I write this. I resisted because I didn't want to offer a substitute for the original workbook. Though I have no substitute to offer, this book builds on that foundation. I have sought to practice *living prayer* for these thirty-five years since the original workbook was published. My conclusion is that the primary dynamic of living prayer is *abiding in Christ*, and that's the theme of this book. As you read this book, you will also notice references to my book *Alive in Christ*, so in a sense this workbook is a sequel to both books.

Nathaniel Hawthorne once thought about writing a story in which the main character never appeared. Unfortunately, this image is too close to the truth of many Christians' lives. We live "stories" in which the "main character" seldom, if ever, appears. He certainly isn't the primary actor in our "story."

Christianity is Christ. He came not only to save us from our sins but also to be an indwelling presence, to shape us into his likeness. He is not to be an infrequent guest, one we invite only to share special occasions. The primary dynamic of the Christian life is *abiding in Christ*. I define *spiritual formation* as "that dynamic process of receiving through faith and appropriating through commitment, discipline, and action, the living Christ into our own life to the end that our life will conform to and manifest the reality of Christ's presence in the world" (*Alive in Christ*, 24). Prayer, then, or *living prayer*, is recognizing, cultivating awareness of, and giving expression to the indwelling Christ (ibid., 27).

The gracious invitation of Christ is "abide in me." The prayer of the writer of Ephesians was "that Christ may dwell in your hearts through faith, as you are being rooted and grounded in love" (3:17). The idea of abiding in Christ offers stupendous possibility, and it should be the mark of *normal* Christian living. Thanks for joining me in exploring that possibility in this workbook.

HOW TO USE THE WORKBOOK

This workbook, designed for individual and group use, calls for an eight-week commitment. We ask you to commit about thirty minutes each day to read, reflect, record, and pray. Hopefully, those thirty minutes will come at the beginning of the day. However, if you can't devote thirty minutes in the morning, spend thirty minutes whenever you have time during the day; the important thing is to engage with this book regularly—daily. This is not simply a study; it is a spiritual journey, the purpose of which is to assimilate the content into your daily life. The journey is personal, though we hope you will share your insights and responses with several others who will meet together once a week during the eight weeks of the adventure.

The workbook is arranged in eight major divisions, each designed to guide you for one week. Each week has seven daily sections containing three sections: (1) reading, (2) reflecting and recording thoughts about the material and your understanding and experience, and (3) practical suggestions for weaving ideas from reading and reflecting in your daily life. Because I believe that we can't be persons of prayer without being persons of the Word, each day begins with a portion of scripture, and the reading and reflecting are punctuated with scripture.

Throughout the workbook you will see this symbol:

When you come to that symbol, please stop. Do not read further. Reflect as requested so that you will internalize the ideas shared or the experience reflected upon.

REFLECTING AND RECORDING

After the reading each day, you are asked to record some of your reflections. The degree of meaning you receive from this workbook depends largely on your faithfulness in practicing its method. You may be unable on a particular day to do precisely what is requested. If so, simply record that fact and note why you can't follow through. On some days there will be more suggestions than you can deal with in the time you have available. Do what is most meaningful for you, and do not feel guilty about the rest.

Always remember that this pilgrimage is personal. What you write in your workbook is your private property. For this reason, I do not recommend sharing the workbook. Each person needs his or her own copy. The importance of what you write is not what it may mean to someone else but what it means to you. Writing, even if only brief notes or single-word reminders, helps you clarify your thoughts and feelings and solidify your decisions and commitments.

The significance of the reflecting and recording dimension will grow as you move along. Even after the eight weeks, you will find meaning in looking back to what you wrote on a particular day in response to a particular situation.

SHARING THE JOURNEY WITH OTHERS

The value of this workbook is enhanced if you share the adventure with eight to twelve other persons. Larger numbers tend to limit individual involvement. If you decide to use the workbook in a larger group, such as a Sunday school class, be intentional about having time to share in smaller groups. In this way you will profit from the insights of others, and they will profit from yours. This book includes a guide for group meetings at the end of each week.

If a group is working through this workbook together, everyone should begin the workbook on the same day so that when your group meets, all will have dealt with the same material and will be at the same place in the text. Beginning the adventure with an initial get-acquainted group meeting is a good idea. This introduction provides a guide for the initial meeting.

Group sessions are designed to last one and one-half hours (except the initial meeting). Participants covenant to attend all sessions unless an emergency prevents. There will be eight weekly sessions in addition to the get-acquainted meeting.

GROUP LEADER'S TASKS

One person may provide the leadership for the entire eight weeks, or leaders may be assigned from week to week. The leader's tasks include the following:

1. Read the Group Meeting directions at the end of each week and determine ahead of time how to handle the session. You may not be able to use all the suggestions for sharing and praying together. Select those you think will be most meaningful and for which you have adequate time.
2. Model a style of openness, honesty, and warmth. Do not pressure anyone to share. As the leader, be willing to be the first one to share, especially personal experiences.

3. Moderate the discussion.
4. Encourage reluctant members to participate; avoid letting a few group members dominate the conversation.
5. Keep the sharing centered in personal experience rather than on academic debate.
6. Honor the time schedule. If it appears necessary to go longer than one and one-half hours, get the group's consensus for continuing another twenty or thirty minutes.
7. Be sure the entire group knows the meeting time and place, especially if meetings are held in different homes.
8. See that the necessary materials for meetings are available and that the meeting room is arranged ahead of time.

Holding weekly meetings in the homes of participants is a good idea. (Hosts or hostesses, make sure there are as few interruptions as possible from children, telephones, pets, and so forth.) If the meetings are held in a church, plan to meet in an informal setting. Encourage participants to dress casually.

If refreshments are planned, serve them after the formal meeting. This will allow individuals who wish to stay longer for informal discussion to do so, while those who need to may leave, having had the full value of the meeting time.

SUGGESTIONS FOR INITIAL GET-ACQUAINTED MEETING

Leader: Read the introduction before the meeting. The initial meeting has two purposes: getting acquainted and beginning the shared pilgrimage. Here are ideas for getting started:

1. Ask each person in the group to give his or her full name and the name by which each wishes to be called. Address everyone by first name or nickname. If name tags are needed, provide them.
2. Let each person in the group share one happy, exciting, or meaningful experience during the past three or four weeks.
3. Ask any who are willing to share their expectations of this workbook study. Why did they become a part of the group study? What does each one expect to gain from it? What are his or her reservations?
4. Review the introduction and ask if anyone has questions about how to use this book. If group members have not received copies of the workbook, hand out the books now. Remember that everyone must have a workbook.
5. Day 1 in the workbook is the day after this initial meeting; the next meeting should be held on Day 7 of the first week. If the group must choose a weekly meeting time other

than seven days from this initial session, adjust the weekly reading assignment so that the weekly meetings occur on Day 7, and Day 1 is the day after a group meeting.

6. Nothing binds group members together more than praying for one another. Encourage everyone to write all group members' names in their workbook and to pray for each one by name daily during the eight weeks.
7. After announcing the time and place of the next meeting, close with a prayer, thanking God for each person in the group, for the opportunity for growth, and for the possibility of growing through spiritual disciplines.

God bless you as you continue this workbook journey.

REHEARSING THE GOSPEL

Day 1

TO GOD BE THE GLORY

Shout for joy to the LORD, all the earth.
Worship the Lord with gladness;
come before him with joyful songs.
Know that the LORD is God.
It is he who made us, and we are his;
we are his people, the sheep of his pasture.

Enter his gates with thanksgiving
and his courts with praise;
give thanks to him and praise his name.
For the LORD is good and his love endures forever;
his faithfulness continues through all generations. (Psalm 100, NIV)

Johann Sebastian Bach, the man whose music has come to be called the Fifth Gospel, once said, "All music should have no other end and aim than the glory of God and the soul's refreshment; where this is not remembered there is no real music but only a devilish hubbub." He headed his compositions with the letters *J.J, Jesus Juva*, which means "Jesus, help me." He ended them *S.D.G, Soli Dei gratia*, which means, "To God alone be the glory." (www.firstpres-byonline/org/Portals/1409)

To God alone be the glory! Why? Because of who God is. Read again Psalm 100.

(Whenever you see this sign, pause to follow the instruction given.)

Seek to feel the psalmist's emotions. He is full of awe and gratitude. Let these words sink in. "The LORD is God . . . it is he who made us . . . we are his people, the sheep of his pasture. . . . The LORD is good and his love endures forever; his faithfulness continues through all generations" (NIV).

It matters whether or not we believe in God. But far more important is what we believe *about* God. That should be unquestionably clear to us. For decades, and more intensely during the wars in Iraq and Afghanistan, the news has been filled with stories of suicide bombers killing those who do not believe as they do ("infidels," they call them). They believe that because they sacrifice their own lives, they will immediately enter into paradise.

What we believe about God matters. At a level far less dramatic than extreme jihadists, it matters. Scripture is clear about it. Creation, the Fall, the Incarnation, the teaching of Jesus, the Cross, and the Resurrection—the movement of God in all of these events is a movement of grace. When we fully claim God's grace, it transforms us.

As unbelievable as it may appear on the surface, this proclamation is the heart of the gospel: *I am loved by God.* My favorite way of stating it is this: There is a place in God's heart that only I can fill—only you can fill. To deny this truth is to commit the great sin of disbelief. God's desire for a relationship with us is declared on boldfaced billboards visible from almost any location in the Bible.

The prophet Isaiah pronounced God's judgment on Israel but constantly reminded the Israelites of God's extravagant love. "The LORD longs to be gracious to you; he rises to show you compassion" (Isa. 30:18, NIV). Think about it. The Lord, "high and lifted up" (Isa. 6:1, KJV), as Isaiah describes God—the Creator of all that is, the King of the universe—longs to offer you and me compassion and grace. All we need to do is take one step toward God—turn our minds and hearts in God's direction, and God welcomes us with compassion.

And what about Jesus? The Gospel of John expresses it clearly. "The Word became flesh and made his dwelling among us. We have seen his glory, the glory of the One and Only, who came from the Father, full of grace and truth" (1:14, NIV).

Full of grace. Wow! So Jesus forgives sinners, embraces prodigals, reaches out to embrace those whom others reject—the immigrant, the prostitute, the poor, the prisoner. He heals the broken, seeks the lost, and frees those in prisons and others who are bound. Grace redeems, restores, and re-creates. No wonder Bach signed his compositions, "To God be the glory"!

REFLECTING AND RECORDING

Reflect for a moment on this claim: It matters whether or not we believe in God. But far more important is what we believe *about* God.

Make a list of words you would use to describe God.

Go back over the list and put a check beside those words that support the claim that the primary characteristics of God are love and grace.

Spend the rest of your time reflecting on this claim about prayer: *God is good, and communication with God is possible.* (Note: This is the principal theme of *The Workbook of Living Prayer.*) Look at prayer as you have practiced it. Has it been rooted in the conviction that God is good? Do you have any difficulty believing that communication with God is possible?

DURING THE DAY

"There is a place in God's heart that only I can fill" is printed on page 203. Cut out this affirmation and put it somewhere you will see it every day this week (on your bathroom mirror, breakfast table, car dashboard). Remind yourself of this truth often throughout the day.

Day 2

IRRESISTIBLE INVITATION

When the woman saw that the fruit of the tree was good for food and pleasing to the eye, and also desirable for gaining wisdom, she took some and ate it. She also gave some to her husband, who was with her, and he ate it. Then the eyes of both of them were opened, and they realized they were naked; so they sewed fig leaves together and made coverings for themselves.

Then the man and his wife heard the sound of the Lord God as he was walking in the garden in the cool of the day, and they hid from the Lord God among the trees of the garden. But the Lord God called to the man, "Where are you?" (Gen. 3:6-9, NIV)

The title of the book I wrote just before this one is *Irresistible Invitation.* The editors and I struggled with that title. When you read the title, perhaps you thought, *How can an invitation be irresistible? I am free to respond however I choose to any invitation I receive.* I wrestled with the same thoughts and feelings. Then I went to the dictionary and found this definition: "Irresistible: impossible to successfully resist."

That definition diminished my reservations. Of course we are free; we can resist. But we can't successfully resist God's incredible grace. As creatures made in the image of God, we can't *successfully* disregard the extravagant heart of God. As clear as anything else in the Bible is the fact that God seeks us. That's the story line of scripture—a searching God who takes the initiative. Even our praying is a response to God's grace.

It makes our hearts beat faster—to realize that God offers us an incredible invitation, a personal invitation, made unconditional with the seal of the cross. It boggles the mind—to think that the One who sketched out the first atom, hung the stars in place, crafted creation in magnificent glory, and breathed into us creatures who are in his image, the breath of life—that this Mighty One, the Creator of all that is, would invite us into a personal relationship. God's invitation is not a onetime event, nor does it come as a onetime first-class delivery note. The invitation is for an ongoing relationship, and it constantly invades our awareness.

It all began with Adam and Eve in the Garden. When they sinned, they experienced guilt. They did not want to see God or for God to see them, so they hid. But God came looking for them, calling, "Adam, Eve, where are you?" Jonah hid from God on a ship. He didn't want God to find him because he was running away from what God was asking him to do. The story goes on: Elijah hid in a cave; Peter tried to hide his Galilean accent from those around the fire in the courtyard where Jesus was on trial.

This is the story recorded in scripture: people hiding, God seeking. Jesus underscored the theme in his parables of the lost coin, the lost sheep, and the lost son (found in Luke 15, which is sometimes called the gospel within the Gospel). Most of us thought the Bible was the story about people seeking God. Not so. It's the story of God seeking us.

In my devotional time recently, I came across a verse I had never noticed before: "After you have suffered for a little while, the God of all grace, who has called you to his eternal glory in Christ, will himself restore, support, strengthen, and establish you" (1 Pet. 5:10).

Don't you like that? *"The God of all grace."* That is who God is—a seeking God who calls us into his eternal glory in Christ. He will forgive and redeem. He will restore. He will support. He will strengthen us. I like the way J. B. Phillips translates Paul's word in Philippians 4:13. You probably memorized that verse this way: "I can do all things through [Christ] who strengthens me." Phillips doesn't render it as "I can do all things" but as "I am ready for anything through the strength of the One who lives within me."*

Our God is a seeking God, the God of all grace.

REFLECTING AND RECORDING

Spend two or three minutes reflecting on this claim: We can resist, but we can't successfully resist God's incredible grace.

Look back over the list of words you made yesterday to describe God. How does that list match with the notion that *our God is a seeking God, the God of all grace*?

Yesterday we noted this foundational principle of prayer: God is good, and communication with God is possible. Here is a second principle: *Prayer is a response to God's grace.* How does that idea fit with the way you have been praying?

Memorization is a helpful spiritual discipline—not simply the process but appropriating something in your mind that you can call upon as a source of strength, guidance, and inspiration. While this is especially true of scripture, it is also true of hymns. The following stanza is a poetic expression of our focus today.

> I sought the Lord, and afterward I knew
> he moved my soul to seek him, seeking me,
> It was not I that found, O Savior true;
> no, I was found of thee. (Anonymous, *The United Methodist Hymnal*, no. 341)

Spend the rest of your time seeking to memorize this verse. If you think you are not good at memorization, don't let this prevent you from trying. Take it two lines at a time, reading those lines five or six times; then do the same thing with the next two lines. It will amaze you how much will live in your mind if you will mull over the lines.

DURING THE DAY

Continue paying regular attention to the message on yesterday's cutout: There is a place in God's heart that only I can fill.

If you memorized the hymn stanza, make a point to quote it at least two or three times today. If you have not memorized it, if possible refer to your workbook sometime during the day to continue the memorization process.

Day 3

THE INCARNATION

> He is the image of the invisible God, the firstborn of all creation; for in him all things in heaven and on earth were created, things visible and invisible, whether thrones or dominions or rulers or powers—all things have been created through him and for him. He himself is before all things, and in him all things hold together. He is the head of the body, the church; he is the beginning, the firstborn from the dead, so that he might come to have first place in everything. For in him all the fullness of God was pleased to dwell, and through him God was pleased to reconcile to himself all things, whether on earth or in heaven, by making peace through the blood of his cross. (Colossians 1:15-20)

The dictionary defines *essence* as "the distinctive quality or qualities of something . . . that which makes something what it is." In this first week of our workbook journey, we center on the essence of the gospel.

This is Christianity's unique claim: God has come to us in Jesus Christ. We call it incarnation. In the two verses preceding the ones quoted above, Paul encapsulated the essence of God's saving work in Jesus Christ: "[God] has rescued us from the power of darkness and transferred us into the kingdom of his beloved Son, in whom we have redemption, the forgiveness of sins" (Col. 1:13-14). Having sounded this astounding good news, Paul felt it wise to tell us who this Son really is, into whose kingdom we have been brought. "[Christ] is the image of the invisible God, the firstborn of all creation; for in him all things in heaven and on earth were created, things visible and invisible, whether thrones or dominions or rulers or powers—all things have been created through him and for him."

Incredible! God's ultimate revelation is Jesus. Let me put it in contrast. Few leaders in the twentieth century seemed as immortal as Mao Tse-tung. Chairman Mao became the incarnation of a movement, a system of thought, and a revolution that impacted nine hundred million people (the population of China in the 1970s). He lived to be eighty-three and was China's leader for over three decades. Shortly after Mao's death, an admirer wrote: "He conceived of the Chinese revolution, and then helped cause it to happen. And, in the process, the thought of Chairman Mao became inculcated in almost every Chinese. The word almost literally became flesh" (Orville Shell, *In the People's Republic* [New York: Random House, 1977], viii).

Note the conditional word *almost*. "The Word *almost* literally became flesh." John, writing of Jesus, said, "The Word became flesh." No reservation, no conditional definition. And Paul wrote in 2 Corinthians 4:6 that God has shone in our hearts "the light of the knowledge of the glory of God in the face of Jesus Christ."

During the 2008 Olympics, China paraded itself before the world. It was one of the most spectacular demonstrations of national life and vitality television has shown. But there was no reference to Chairman Mao, only a picture of his portrait and tomb.

In Mao, powerful man that he was, the word *almost* became flesh. But with Jesus, the Word did become flesh and dwelt among us. We beheld his glory—the glory of the only begotten Son of the Father. This is the incredibility of the Incarnation—that "the radiant glory of God shines in the face of Jesus Christ" (2 Cor. 4:6, AP). He is the "image of the invisible God."

REFLECTING AND RECORDING

In the space provided on page 19, write your own paraphrase of Colossians 1:15-20. Read the passage several times before you put it in your own words. Don't struggle or ponder about whether you are being true to the text; simply restate what is said in the way you would say it.

DURING THE DAY

Today's primary thought is that the radiant glory of God shines in the face of Jesus Christ. We call it *incarnation*. Seek out at least two persons today to tell that you are on this workbook journey and that today you are thinking about the Incarnation. See how they respond to the fact that Jesus is the image of the invisible God.

Day 4

THE IMAGE OF GOD

> For in him the complete being of God, by God's own choice, came to dwell. Through him God chose to reconcile the whole universe to himself, making peace through the shedding of his blood upon the cross—to reconcile all things, whether on earth or in heaven, through him alone. (Colossians 1:19-20, NEB)

Paul makes the case for the Incarnation in every way possible. Jesus is the "image of the invisible God . . . in him the complete being of God, by God's own choice, came to dwell" (NEB). The Greek word translated "image" is *eikṓn*, from which we get our word *icon*. An icon was a representation or reproduction with precise likeness. An image of a sovereign or hero on a coin or a portrait of a person's likeness is an icon. That's who Jesus was, Paul is saying—a representation of God. *Eikṓn* also means manifestation. All of us are created in the image of God. Jesus was more than that; he was God in human manifestation. This is not easy to grasp.

Athanasius (c. 293–373), the bishop of Alexandria, was one of the most important persons in early church history. As a young man he took part in the First Council of Nicaea (325), which produced the Nicene Creed, one of the most complete statements of Christian beliefs.

In those early years, and continuing throughout history, the church has been threatened by heresy. One early heresy was Arianism, the false doctrine that Jesus was merely a human being. Along with other great "fathers" of the church, Athanasius effectively opposed this heresy. He championed the doctrine of the Incarnation and in his writings worked to clarify how God became human in the person of Jesus. With profound understanding, but in classical simplicity, Athanasius made the case for the Incarnation by contending that God created us to know him, and Jesus is our way of knowing God.

Athanasius believed that since God created humankind through his own word, God realized that there was no way for persons, owing to the limitation of their nature, to have knowledge of their Creator. So Athanasius made his case beautifully. God, he said,

> took pity on mankind . . . and did not leave them destitute of the knowledge of Himself, lest their very existence should prove purposeless.
>
> For of what use is existence of the creature if it cannot know its Maker? How could

humans be reasonable beings if they had no knowledge of the Word and Reason of the Father, through whom they had received their being? They would be no better than the beasts, had they no knowledge beyond earthly things. And why should God have made them at all, if He had not intended them to know Him? (Quoted in *Devotional Classics*, 339)

So, our good and gracious God came to us in Jesus Christ. At creation, God had given us a share in his own image, but how could we even begin to get a hint of what that means? Now we know that this image in the likeness of which we are created is our Lord Jesus Christ. This is the very core of the Christian gospel.

In 1931 a collection of essays titled *If It Had Happened Otherwise* was published. The essays, some written by leading historians of the time, were written on the premise of what might have been if certain historical events had not happened. What would history be like if Napoleon had escaped to America, if the Moors had won the war in Spain, if John Wilkes Booth had missed when he shot Lincoln, if Lee had won at Gettysburg? Those questions inspire a serious reflection on the biggest what-if of all: *what* if God had not come to us in Jesus Christ?

If God had "stayed at home" and not come to us in Jesus Christ,
 we would not know who God is and what God is like;
 there would be no salvation, no answer to our sin problem;
 there would be no clear and authoritative teaching about God's reign;
 we would have no power over Satan;
 there would be no victory over death, no promise of eternal life.
But God did not stay at home. The Word became flesh.

REFLECTING AND RECORDING

The following is the full statement about Jesus in the Nicene Creed. Read it slowly with pencil in hand. Put a check next to the words that describe Jesus.

We believe in one God,
the Father, the Almighty,
maker of heaven and earth,
of all that is, seen and unseen.

We believe in one Lord, Jesus Christ,
the only Son of God,
eternally begotten of the Father,
God from God, Light from Light,
true God from true God,
begotten, not made,
of one Being with the Father;

through him all things were made.
For us and for our salvation
he came down from heaven,
was incarnate of the Holy Spirit and the Virgin Mary
and became truly human.
For our sake he was crucified under Pontius Pilate;
he suffered death and was buried.
On the third day he rose again
in accordance with the Scriptures;
he ascended into heaven
and is seated at the right hand of the Father.
He will come again in glory
to judge the living and the dead,
and his kingdom will have no end. (*The United Methodist Hymnal*, no. 880)

Now make a list of the characteristics you checked.

Is there anything you would add to the list? Make notes here.

Read again the list of what would be missing if God *had stayed home*, and then offer a prayer of thanksgiving for his coming.

DURING THE DAY

Were you able to engage anyone yesterday in talking about the Incarnation? How did that go? Today, try again with new people, sharing with them the discussion of what things would be like if God had "stayed at home."

Day 5

SALVATION . . . RESCUED

And so, from the day we heard, we have not ceased to pray for you, asking that you may be filled with the knowledge of his will in all spiritual wisdom and understanding, to walk in a manner worthy of the Lord, fully pleasing to him, bearing fruit in every good work and increasing in the knowledge of God. May you be strengthened with all power, according to his glorious might, for all endurance and patience with joy, giving thanks to the Father, who has qualified you to share in the inheritance of the saints in light. He has delivered us from the domain of darkness and transferred us to the kingdom of his beloved Son, in whom we have redemption, the forgiveness of sins. (Colossians 1:9-14, ESV)

My name is Asher Lev, the Asher Lev, about whom you have read in newspapers and magazines, about whom you talk so much at your dinner affairs and cocktail parties. The notorious and legendary Lev of the Brooklyn Crucifixion."

With those words, Chaim Potok begins his novel *My Name is Asher Lev*. It's about a young boy whose extraordinary talent leads him away from his family and his faith into a painful maturity and a perilous success. Asher Lev longs to be a painter, and he pursues this longing despite his father's disapproval. He even paints what he calls the *Brooklyn Crucifixion*—a painting of the crucifixion of Christ.

As an explanation of that, on the very first page of the novel, Asher Lev says, "I am an observant Jew. Yes, of course, observant Jews do not paint crucifixions. As a matter of fact, observant Jews do not paint at all—in the way that I am painting."

Asher persists in his quest to be an artist despite the growing alienation from his parents. One time his guide and teacher says to him: "Art is whether or not there is a scream in him wanting to get out in a special way . . . or a laugh." (Chaim Potok, *My Name Is Asher Lev*, 3, 212)

When I came to Colossians 1:13-14, I thought about these words concerning art. Paul could never get far in any of his writing without expressing what is "screaming inside him," what he is laughing with joy about. This truth of the gospel and inner experience of Paul wants to get out in a special way, and the way it gets out in this one sentence is no less a work of art and a statement of passion than that of a painter who would put it on canvas. "[God] has rescued us from the power of darkness and transferred us into the kingdom of his beloved Son, in whom we have redemption, the forgiveness of sins."

Paul's word is at once a scream and a laugh—a joyful shout, a passionate proclamation about what Christ has done. Look at two powerful words.

First, *rescued.* Paul is saying that as God had rescued the Hebrew people from captivity and oppression in Egypt, so now he has rescued the new Israel from the dark principalities and powers that rule the present world order. Once exiled and without hope, these sojourners from the promise are settled in the kingdom of Christ.

"Rescued from the power of darkness" is one of many images Paul uses for his understanding of a core dimension of the essence of the gospel: justification by grace through faith. We are all in bondage to sin. "There is no one who is righteous, not even one. . . . All have sinned and fall short of the glory of God" (Rom. 3:10, 23). When we are honest, we admit that—how well we know our sin! But God has shown his great love for us by giving us Jesus Christ as a sacrifice, substitute, and power over sin. His death on the cross was death on our behalf. When we receive that sacrificial love by faith, we are justified—made right with God.

Justification is a metaphor from the law courts, so when we think about salvation as justification, the image is that of being on trial. The Greek word translated "to justify" does not mean to *make* one something but to *treat*, to *reckon*, or to *account* someone as something. So here is the picture. When we appear before God, we are anything but innocent. We have sinned; we are estranged; we are guilty. Yet God treats us as if we were innocent. That is what justification means. Through our faith in Jesus Christ, and what God has done for us in Christ, we are justified. It is all a matter of grace, God's gift of love and full acceptance of us.

Paul uses this strong word, *rescued*, to talk about justification. Some translations of this text use the word. The dynamic is freedom. I like the way Eugene Peterson renders the text in *The Message*: "God rescued us from dead-end alleys and dark dungeons. He's set us up in the kingdom of the Son he loves so much, the Son who got us out of the pit we were in, got rid of the sins we were doomed to keep repeating" (Col. 1:13-14).

Rescued, set free
from the ravaging guilt of sin
from neurotic fear of the future that makes us impotent
from bondage to material security
from jealousy that breaks into rage, destroying someone we love
from drug, sexual, and other destructive addictions
from the passionate drive for immediate gratification
from that never-satisfied state of bland living into a life of service, care, and compassion for others.

Isn't this our need? Even though we may have professed our faith and accepted our salvation, don't we continually preoccupy ourselves anxiously with what we ought to be and do? Constantly stirring within us are all sorts of passions, and we waste energy focusing on our efforts to overcome these passions, rather than releasing ourselves to be empowered by Christ—and be delivered by him.

(We will cover the second strong word in Colossians 1 tomorrow.)

REFLECTING AND RECORDING

Sometimes, because of our sin and failure, our feelings of shame and guilt, we question our relationship with Christ and even our "salvation experience." Spend some time reflecting on your spiritual journey. Locate that time or time frame in your life when you began to identify yourself as a Christian. You may have had a specific conversion experience that you can identify by time and place. You may have grown up in a Christian home, and you claimed the Christian faith for yourself over a period of time, maybe years. You may have shared confirmation training in the church and professed for yourself the faith into which you were baptized as an infant.

Our experiences vary. Spend some time now reflecting on your own journey.

Thank God now for his gift of salvation in Jesus Christ.

If you don't remember ever confessing Jesus as Lord and Savior, you may do so right now. All you need to do is pray this prayer with a trusting heart.

> Eternal God, I know I have made a lot of mistakes in my life. I know that I have sinned, but I believe you can wipe the slate clean. I believe you sent your Son, Jesus, to die on the cross for me, and I accept him now as my Savior and Lord. Father, I thank you for drawing me to you, I thank you for your forgiveness, and I thank you for the new life you have begun in me. I believe I am a new creation in Christ Jesus. Amen.

Let someone know that you have prayed this prayer, that you have made specific your Christian commitment. Tell a member of your church or a friend you know is a Christian. It always helps to verbalize to another the decisions we have made.

DURING THE DAY

By now you should have claimed and internalized the truth you have been living with all week: "There is a place in God's heart that only I can fill." Is there someone you know who really needs to believe that truth about himself or herself? If so, call or write a note to the person, sharing that good news.

Day 6

SALVATION . . .TRANSFERRED

> He has rescued us from the domain of darkness, and transferred us to the kingdom of His beloved Son, in whom we have redemption, the forgiveness of sins. (Col. 1:13-14, NASB)

The next strong word in the Colossians text we began considering yesterday is *transferred.* "[God] has transferred us to the kingdom of His beloved Son" (NASB). God's grace delivers us "from the power of darkness." This gift is through Jesus Christ, whom God sent to redeem and forgive us through an all-sufficient sacrifice. We are not only delivered from the power of darkness but also transferred into a new kingdom over which Christ reigns and God's love is freely and fully given.

The New International Version uses the word *brought*, and the King James Version uses the word *translated.* "He has translated us [brought us] into the kingdom of his dear Son." The word was used to describe the deportation of a population from one country to another.

The truth for us is that Jesus did not release us from bondage only to have us wander aimlessly. He moved us into the kingdom of his light and made us victors over Satan's power.

Then Paul said, "In whom we have redemption." The word *redeemed* means to release a prisoner. It may not be easy for us to grasp that image, since most of us have never literally been in jail. The full impact comes when we realize that Paul is speaking autobiographically.

Do you remember how Paul expressed his own struggle in Romans 7, where he anguishes over the civil war that is going on inside him? "I do not understand my own actions. For I do not do what I want, but I do the very thing I hate. . . . I can will what is right, but I cannot do it" (vv. 15, 18). Paul feels he is being brought under the captivity of sin. He groans mournfully, "For I do not do the good I want, but the evil I do not want is what I do. Now if I do what I do not want, it is no longer I that do it, but sin that dwells within me" (vv. 19-20).

You can feel the anguishing turmoil as he cries out, "Wretched man that I am! Who will rescue me from this body of death?"(v. 24). There's that word *rescue* again. Paul answers his own cry. "Thanks be to God through Jesus Christ our Lord!" (v. 25).

That's the way chapter 7 closes (with one more sentence remaining). The first verse of chapter 8 is, "There is therefore now no condemnation for those who are in Christ Jesus." See the dramatic change in Paul's testimony. "Wretched man that I am! Who will rescue me? . . . There is therefore now no condemnation." Does his testimony help us grasp the meaning of salvation? Christ frees us.

Some Christians in Africa translate the New Testament word for *redemption* into the phrase "God took our heads out." A rather strange thought, until you trace it back to the nineteenth-century slave trade; then it becomes powerful. White men invaded African villages and carried men, women, and children off to be sold as slaves. Each person had an iron collar buckled around his or her neck. A chain attached to the collar was attached to the iron collar around the neck of another, and another, and another—until there would be a long chain of persons, driven to the coast and shipped off to be sold as slaves. Sometimes a loved one, a relative or friend, might recognize someone who been captured and offer a ransom to the captors to remove the collar and free the person. Thus the word for redemption: "God took our heads out."(Dunnam, *Irresistible Invitation: Responding to the Extravagant Heart of God* [Abingdon Press, 2008], 157)

However we state it, whatever image we use from our own culture, the word *redemption* means that God's action in Jesus Christ sets us free from the bondage of sin, guilt, and death. The cross is our proof that God has accepted us, and no power in the universe can separate us from his love (see Romans 8:33-38).

REFLECTING AND RECORDING

Spend some time reflecting on freedom as the dynamic of salvation. Read the following questions and put a check mark by any that speak to your present situation.

___ Do you feel pain in your heart, a heaviness of spirit because there is a broken relationship that needs reconciliation?

___ As a parent, do you have children from whom you are estranged?

___ Do you feel helpless because you are bound in the tenacious grip of alcohol, drugs, gambling, pornography, or some other destructive habit?

___ Is your energy drained because you are living too close to the edge of moral compromise?

___ Does your pride often cause you to think more highly of yourself than you ought?

___ Are you holding back a particular area of your life that you have not yet surrendered to God?

Now look at the questions you have checked. In your mind and heart, turn that check mark into a confession, an acknowledgment of your need for redemption. In a prayer of thanksgiving, claim the glorious fact that Christ comes to free us.

DURING THE DAY

Identify three times during this day when you will have the opportunity to pause for just a minute or two. At the designated times, pause and give thanks for the following: *Christ comes to free us.*

DAY 7

THE GOD WHO COMES

> The god of this age has blinded the minds of unbelievers, so that they cannot see the light of the gospel of the glory of Christ, who is the image of God. For we do not preach ourselves, but Jesus Christ as Lord, and ourselves as your servants for Jesus' sake. For God, who said, "Let light shine out of darkness," made his light shine in our hearts to give us the light of the knowledge of the glory of God in the face of Christ. (2 Corinthians 4:4-6, NIV)

It's amazing how the music and words of songs and hymns we grew up on remain embedded in our memory. I believe that as we grow in our faith, the experiences and content of our past that are most relevant to our present emerge from our memory to enhance our journey.

When I am alone—driving, sitting on the beach, walking in the woods—I sometimes find myself breaking into song:

> Jesus, Jesus, Jesus,
> sweetest name I know
> fills my every longing,
> keeps me singing as I go.
> (Luther B. Bridgers, *The United Methodist Hymnal*, no. 380)

This gospel hymn chorus expresses the heart of the gospel.

The whole story of salvation, the story of history, is the story of *the God who comes*. Paul put it this way: "For God, who said, 'Let light shine out of darkness,' made his light shine in our hearts to give us the light of the knowledge of the glory of God in the face of Christ" (2 Cor. 4:6, NIV). The Incarnation brings the world his presence. God is made human in Christ.

God makes himself present to us in such a powerful way that who God is, is now answered emphatically. The invisible, intangible God is now visible and tangible.

If we don't get this in our understanding of the gospel, we won't get the rest. If we don't begin here, there is no place to go. The radiant glory of God shines in the face of Jesus Christ. If Jesus is truly God, then everything is clear. If I cannot believe this, I will muddle along in confusion and darkness. And devastatingly, I will wander alone on my attempted journey of faith.

John S. Dunne, in his *Reasons of the Heart*, offers a challenging word. "Our mind's desire is to know, to understand; but our heart's desire is intimacy, to be known, to be understood. To see God with our mind would be to know God, to understand God; but to see God with our heart would be to have a sense of being known by God, of being understood by God" (Dunne, *Reasons of the Heart*, 39).

We talk about becoming Christian in ways like "being born again," "accepting Christ as Savior," and "inviting Christ into our lives." On the two previous days we focused on two words, *rescued* and *transferred*, to describe the dynamic of salvation. Whatever our language, the faith and experience is that as we confess and repent of our sins, we are forgiven. We are justified, accepted by, and enter into a new relationship with God, who then lives in us by the power of the Holy Spirit as the indwelling Christ. Recall the J. B. Phillips translation of Philippians 4:13: "I am ready for anything through the strength of the one who lives within me."*

Our need to know God with our minds and our hearts is met in the God who has come to us in Jesus Christ. Our desire to know (our minds) is satisfied by God showing us clearly who he is in Jesus Christ. Our desire for intimacy (our hearts) is satisfied in Christ "alive in us" in an ongoing way by the power of the Holy Spirit.

In *Alive in Christ*, I defined spiritual formation as the "dynamic process of receiving through faith and appropriating through commitment, discipline, and action, the living Christ into our own life to the end that our life will conform to, and manifest the reality of Christ's presence in the world" (Dunnam, *Alive in Christ*, 26).

Prayer, then, or prayerful living, "*is recognizing, cultivating awareness of, and giving expression to the indwelling Christ.*" Our living and praying, which cannot be separated, is simply, and profoundly, *abiding in Christ.* That is what this workbook journey is all about.

The saints of the ages have talked most about the living Christ or the *indwelling Christ*, as a "companion along our ways." Thérèse of Lisieux confessed that her final retreat before taking her lifelong vows as a nun was a time of desolation rather than a time of consolation and joy. Her soul felt dry. "Absolute aridity and total abandonment were my lot," she wrote. " I am far from being a saint, and what I have just said is proof of this." Yet, she said, "God showed me clearly . . . the way to please Him."

After her confession, she claimed a word of scripture: "The Lord knoweth our frame. He remembereth that we are dust," and concluded:

> I have frequently noticed that Jesus doesn't want me to lay up provisions; He nourishes me at each moment with a totally new food; I find it within me without my knowing how it is there. I believe it is Jesus Himself hidden in the depths of my poor little heart; He is giving me the grace of acting within me, making me think of all He desires me to do at the present moment. (Thérèse of Lisieux, *Story of a Soul*, 165)

REFLECTING AND RECORDING

Read again, slowly and reflectively, the paragraph quoting John Dunne's *Reasons of the Heart*.

Spend some time thinking about the difference between knowing God with the mind and with the heart.

Think back over this past week. What new insights did you have? What issues brought the most questions? How were you challenged? Did you disagree with any content of the daily readings? What meant the most to you? Make some notes in the space below.

If you are sharing this workbook journey with a group, pray for those persons with whom you will be meeting today. Pray that the group will bond and become a meaningful fellowship.

DURING THE DAY

If you are participating in a group, read the directions on the next three pages for your weekly meeting so that you will be clear about the expectations.

GROUP MEETING FOR WEEK ONE

INTRODUCTION

Group sessions are most effective when all participants talk about their experiences. This guide is designed to facilitate personal sharing. Therefore, you need not be rigid in following these suggestions. The leader especially needs to be sensitive to what is happening in participants' lives and to focus the group's sharing of those experiences in light of that knowledge. We need to respect the ideas of others, listen attentively, and wrestle with new ideas, especially those with which we disagree. The group meeting should not become a debate. Emphasize the experiences and feelings of individuals. While the *content* of the study is important, applying the content to our lives and our relationship with God and others needs priority.

As the persons begin to talk honestly and openly about what is happening in their lives, group meetings will become more meaningful. This means persons should share not only the good and positive but also struggles and difficulties.

This process of group sharing is not easy; it is deceptive to pretend it is. Growth requires effort and struggle. Don't be afraid to share your questions, reservations, and "dry periods."

SHARING TOGETHER

1. Begin your meeting by allowing each person to share the most meaningful day with the workbook this week. The leader should begin this sharing. Tell why that particular day was so meaningful.
2. Next, share your most difficult day with the material, describing what you experienced that was difficult.
3. Invite any two persons who are willing to share their lists of words they use to describe God, and notice how many of those words support the claim that the primary characteristics of God are love and grace. Then spend a few minutes allowing the group to discuss the notion that love and grace are the primary characteristics of God.
4. Spend a few minutes talking about the claim *We can resist, but we can't successfully resist God's incredible grace.*
5. Ask a volunteer to read his or her paraphrase of Colossians 1:15-20 (Reflecting and Recording, Day 3).

6. Invite one or two persons to share their experience of sharing with a person about their workbook journey and the Incarnation (During the Day, Day 3).
7. Invite the group to go to the Reflecting and Recording section of Day 4, and read together the portion of the Nicene Creed printed there. Then discuss how Jesus is described there, if it is a complete definition, and what you might add.
8. Spend some time together talking about salvation in terms of the two words, *rescued* and *transferred.* Invite individuals to share how their experience confirms this understanding of salvation.
9. Before moving into a time of prayer, ask group members if there is any idea, issue, or question raised in this week's content they would like to discuss. Be sensitive to time. If you don't have enough time to finish the discussion, reserve time for completing the discussion at next week's gathering.

PRAYING TOGETHER

Each week's suggestions call for the group to pray together. Corporate prayer empowers Christians. This is a "living prayer" journey, so this dimension of prayer in a shared pilgrimage is important.

Group members need to feel comfortable during corporate prayer. No one should feel pressured to pray aloud. Silent corporate prayer may be as vital and meaningful as spoken prayer. Times of silence, when thinking is centered and attention is focused, may provide our deepest periods of prayer.

Verbalizing thoughts and feelings to God in the presence of fellow pilgrims can be a powerful bonding experience for a group sharing a common journey. Verbal prayers may be offered spontaneously as persons choose to pray aloud. Avoid suggesting, "Let's go around the circle now, and each one pray."

Suggestions are given each week for this "praying together" time. ***Leader***, regard these only as suggestions. What happens in the meeting—the mood, the needs expressed, the timing—should determine the direction of the group's prayer time together. Here are some possibilities for this closing period.

1. Encourage everyone to write the names of group members in the front of their workbook and to pray for them every week.
2. Invite the group to spend a few minutes in silent prayer—three or four minutes is a long time for people who are together for the first time. Ask the group to deliberately think of each person in the group, and what each person may have shared, and pray silently for each person.

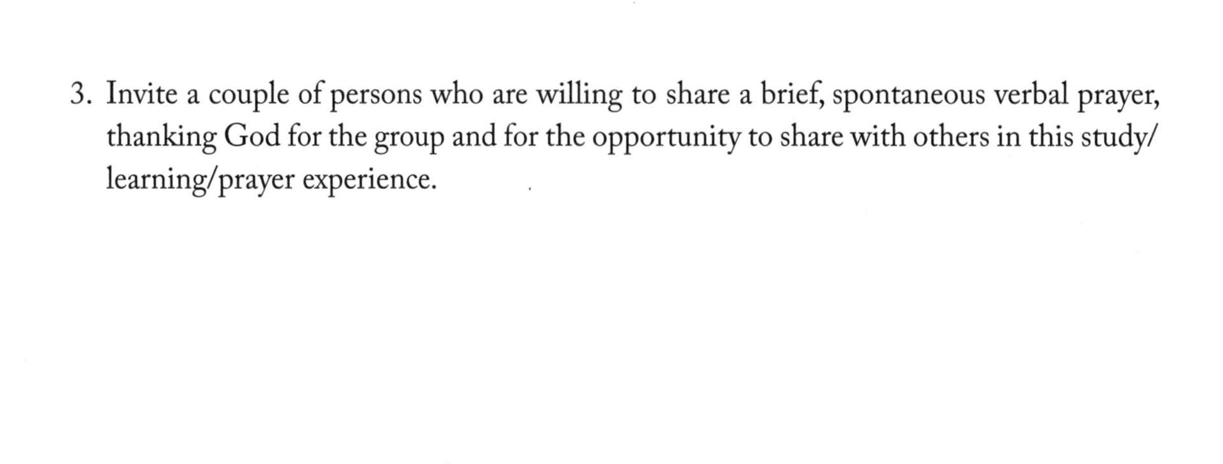

3. Invite a couple of persons who are willing to share a brief, spontaneous verbal prayer, thanking God for the group and for the opportunity to share with others in this study/learning/prayer experience.

PREDICAMENT AND POSSIBILITY

Day 1

GIVING ALL TO CHRIST

> If we have been united with him in a death like his, we will certainly be united with him in a resurrection like his. We know that our old self was crucified with him so that the body of sin might be destroyed, and we might no longer be enslaved to sin. For whoever has died is freed from sin. But if we have died with Christ, we believe that we will also live with him. We know that Christ, being raised from the dead, will never die again; death no longer has dominion over him. The death he died, he died to sin, once for all; but the life he lives, he lives to God. So you also must consider yourselves dead to sin and alive to God in Christ Jesus. (Romans 6:5-11)

To be a Christian is to change. It is to become new. It is not simply a matter of choosing a new lifestyle, though there is a new style. It has to do with becoming a new person.

This is not the way we normally think. C. S. Lewis discusses the all-too-prevalent idea persons have about being Christian before they become Christian. He says we start with our ordinary self—with our own wants and interests.

> We then admit that something else—call it "morality" or "decent behavior," or "the good of society"—has claims on this self: claims which interfere with its own desires. What we mean by "being good" is giving in to those claims. Some of the things the ordinary self wanted to do turn out to be what we call "wrong": well, we must give them up. Other things . . . turn out to be what we call "right": well, we shall have to do them. But we are hoping all the time that when all the demands have been met, the poor natural self will still have some chance, and some time, to get on with its own life and do what it likes.

Spend a few minutes considering Lewis's description. Did you ever think in this fashion? Does any of your present thinking match these ideas?

After his description of the idea we have about being Christian as we contemplate becoming Christian, Lewis concludes,

> As long as we are thinking that way, one or other of two results is likely to follow. Either we give up trying to be good, or else we become very unhappy indeed. (*Lewis,* Mere Christianity, *166–67*)

Spend a few minutes considering this conclusion. Is Lewis right? Have you experienced what he is talking about? Have you seen that dynamic at work in others?

Return to my beginning claim. To be a Christian is to change. It is to become new. It is not simply a matter of choosing a new lifestyle, though there is a new style. It has to do with becoming a new person. The new person is a *person in Christ.*

In Rehearsing the Gospel, Week 1, we considered the dynamic of our becoming Christian as being rescued—set free, and transferred—moved from a domain of darkness into "the kingdom of [God's] beloved Son, in whom we have redemption, the forgiveness of sins." In his letter to the Romans, Paul combined both these dynamics, rescued and transferred, and called us to consider ourselves dead to sin and alive to God in Jesus Christ.

Death and resurrection are the most definitive descriptions of the nature of our becoming Christians and living the Christian life. The life, death, and resurrection of Jesus were the greatest outpouring of God's love and mercy the world has ever known. In Jesus Christ, we are "made right" in our relationship to God. Our sin and guilt is cancelled by his death on the cross. While this is true, that the power of sin is broken by Christ and our sin forgiven, to fully claim our redemption and participate wholly in God's new creation is our lifetime journey. When Paul talked about the death of Christ and our participation in that death, he was thinking not only of forgiveness of past sins, but of a drastic break with sin, a demolishing of sin's dominion over our lives.

So, being crucified with Christ was an experiential fact for Paul, and it must also be for us. We usually think of that primarily in terms of *pardon*, and it is that. That is what our cardinal doctrine of justification by grace through faith underscores. But it is more than pardon; it is *power*. For Paul, it was a matter of death and resurrection. We are no longer "enslaved to sin."

Return to Lewis's discussion of the ordinary idea many folks have about becoming a Christian. The Christian life is completely different, he says: harder and easier.

> Christ says, "Give me All. I don't want so much of your time and so much of your money and so much of your work: I want You. I have not come to torment your natural self, but to kill it. No half-measures are any good. I don't want to cut off a branch here and a branch there, I want to have the whole tree down. . . . Hand over the whole natural self, all the desires which you think innocent as well as the ones you think wicked—the whole outfit. I will give you a new self instead. In fact, I will give you Myself." (*Mere Christianity*, 167)

Being Christian means being a new person united with Christ. In our relationship to God in Jesus Christ we are new persons. Now the life we live must be brought into harmony with our new relationship, our new position in relation to God. Again, Lewis has a challenging image for us: the egg. He says, "It may be hard for an egg to turn into a bird," but it would be immensely harder for it to fly while "remaining an egg." At present, we are somewhat like eggs. But we can't go on forever "being just an ordinary, decent egg. We must be hatched or go bad."

REFLECTING AND RECORDING

Spend two or three minutes reflecting on Lewis's paraphrase of Jesus' word to us: "I have not come to torment your natural self, but to kill it."

Now spend two or three minutes reflecting on my claim: To be a Christian is to change. It is to become new. It is not simply a matter of choosing a new lifestyle, though there is a new style. It has to do with becoming a new person. The new person is a *person in Christ.*

Spend the balance of your time answering this question: In light of the two previous reflection statements, where am I on my Christian journey?

DURING THE DAY

Christ says, "Give me your all." Take this word with you into the day. Call it to mind as often as possible and ask yourself, "What does this mean to me *right now*?"

DAY 2

CHRIST'S LORDSHIP IS NOT OPTIONAL FOR CHRISTIANS

> Very truly, I tell you, unless a grain of wheat falls into the earth and dies, it remains just a single grain; but if it dies, it bears much fruit. Those who love their life lose it, and those who hate their life in this world will keep it for eternal life. Whoever serves me must follow me, and where I am, there will my servant be also. Whoever serves me, the Father will honor. (John 12:24-26)

It has been only during the past twenty-five years, out of fifty years of ministry, that I have been convicted of the common distortion we in the church make in thinking and talking about discipleship. We talk and act as though "discipleship" is a special vocation to which some Christians are called, while the masses may live as Christians without this "deeper level" of commitment or devotion.

We even have those who say that Jesus might be our Savior but not our Lord. There might be some truth in that, but it is a distortion, missing the fullness of the salvation that is ours in Jesus Christ. The Lordship of Christ is not optional for Christians. We may talk about the person and work of Christ in terms of being our Savior and our Lord. As Savior: dying for our salvation. As Lord: present in our life as an empowering, guiding, and comforting presence. But this does not mean we may have one part of the work of Christ without the other. Jesus cannot be our Savior without being our Lord.

Some would describe discipleship as the process of making Jesus Lord of our lives. Again, there is some truth in that. But the problem comes when we act as though there is a difference between being a Christian and being a disciple. That suggests that you can be a Christian without having any intention of following Christ as a disciple. This notion has too often pervaded our understanding of church membership; thus churches are filled with "undisciplined disciples." I believe with Dallas Willard, popular writer and one of the most convincing apologists of the Christian faith, that most problems in contemporary churches can be explained by the fact that members have not yet decided to follow Christ.

Willard makes the case that while there are great costs to being disciples, "the cost of nondiscipleship is far greater—even when this life alone is considered—than the price paid to walk with Jesus." Willard continues:

> Nondiscipleship costs abiding peace, a life penetrated throughout by love, faith that sees everything in the light of God's overriding governance for good, hopefulness that stands firm in the most discouraging of circumstances, power to do what is right and withstand the forces of evil. In short, it costs exactly that abundance of life Jesus said he came to bring. (*The Spirit of the Disciplines*, 263)

The call of Christ is to follow. Following him is not optional for Christians. It may be that our confusion about Jesus as Savior and Lord, or our tendency to separate the work of Christ according to these titles, is a result of our disregarding the most thrilling possibility that is ours: to abide in Christ.

Herein is a problem. There is a difference between *following* Christ and *being in* Christ. While distorting what it means to be a disciple, we have emphasized following Christ as the heart of Christianity, ignoring the dynamic of abiding in Christ. In doing so, we tend to reduce Christianity to a religion of morals and ethics, thus stripping it of its power.

Following Jesus is a nonnegotiable principle for Christians. We cannot follow Jesus for long unless we are *in Christ*, abiding in him. We renew our strength, find direction, and gain confidence by cultivating the presence of Christ within—through prayer, immersing ourselves in scripture, and spending time with God's people so that we act—*we follow*—from the depths of abiding in Christ.

We cultivate the presence of the indwelling Christ to the point that his power prevails and gives us the strength to continue when our own strength would fail. We survive the *doing* of our Christianity by keeping the *being* of our Christian life intact and up-to-date.

REFLECTING AND RECORDING

Spend a few minutes thinking about the distinction between Jesus as Savior and Jesus as Lord.

Examine your own understanding. Is it possible to be a Christian without being a disciple? Do your friends and fellow church members think there is a distinction between the words *Christian* and *disciple*?

Write a few sentences about your understanding of *following* Christ and being *in* Christ.

DURING THE DAY

On page 203 is a prayer that invites Christ to be Lord of our life. Cut it out, carry it with you, or put it somewhere you will see it often during the day. Pray it now, and seek to pray it at least three times during this day.

Sometime today, find someone you trust—someone you consider a growing Christian—and ask that person what distinction he or she makes between *following* Christ and being *in* Christ.

DAY 3

DEAD IN TRESPASSES AND SINS

> As for you, you were dead in your transgressions and sins, in which you used to live when you followed the ways of this world and of the ruler of the kingdom of the air, the spirit who is now at work in those who are disobedient. All of us also lived among them at one time, gratifying the cravings of our sinful nature and following its desires and thoughts. Like the rest, we were by nature objects of wrath. But because of his great love for us, God, who is rich in mercy, made us alive with Christ even when we were dead in transgressions—it is by grace you have been saved. And God raised us up with Christ and seated us with him in the heavenly realms in Christ Jesus, in order that in the coming ages he might show the incomparable riches of his grace, expressed in his kindness to us in Christ Jesus. (Ephesians 2:1-7, NIV)

You can't miss what Paul is saying. He minces no words. "You were dead in your transgressions and sins." Death and sin are taken seriously in the Bible, and they go together. "The wages of sin is death" (Rom. 6:23), contends Paul. In biblical times death had a finality that has been dropped in our modern minds. The immortality of the soul as a natural birthright for humans is an idea foreign to the Bible. It was a Greek concept that crept into our thinking. Death was death in biblical understanding, and only God could do anything about it. What happens to us after death is completely dependent upon how we stand before God and what God chooses to do.

Because of sin, Paul says, we are dead. Sin cuts us off from God, the source of life. Paul names three characteristics of the human predicament.

1. We are controlled by Satan: *"You followed . . . the ruler of the kingdom of the air, the spirit who is now at work in those who are disobedient."* The "ruler of the kingdom of the air" is a title for Satan. As we noted on Day 6 of Week 1, the unredeemed world is described as the "domain of darkness" (Col. 1:13, NASB), and salvation means being rescued from that domain.

2. Apart from Christ, yet unredeemed, we *"followed the ways of this world . . . gratifying the cravings of our sinful nature."* Apart from Christ, we are pulled to conform to the standards of a world without regard for the demands of our God of love, righteousness, peace, and justice, a God who calls us "to be holy as I am holy" (Lev. 19:2).

3. When we gratify our sinful nature, we become children of wrath. The writer of Ephesians uses another picture—*hardness of heart*: "They are darkened in their understanding and separated from the life of God because of the ignorance that is in them due to the hardening of their hearts" (4:19, NIV). He says they will come to a place where they are past feeling, or "having lost all sensitivity" (v. 19). The Greek word translated "hardening" is *pōrōsis*, coming from *pōrōs*, which described a stone that is harder than marble. The popular New Testament scholar William Barclay renders the word as "petrifying," making vivid the fact that as "dead in sin" we are absolutely void of all spiritual life, and by our very nature, objects of God's wrath (Barclay, *The Letters to the Galatians and Ephesians*, 175).

We have gone through a long period, even in the church, when to talk about sin and alienation from God was viewed as old-fashioned, quaint; for some "as Victorian as crinoline." The flowering of the "personal growth" movement in America brought a major shift in the vocabulary of the human condition. *Fulfillment, potential, self-actualization, self-expression,* and *personal growth* overshadowed words like *sin, repentance, confession, estrangement*, and *fractured* as descriptive of human reality. A pervasive optimism about human nature prevailed in our language and to a marked degree in the preaching and teaching of the church.

Some mainline Protestants get queasy about the biblical picture of salvation. H. Richard Niebuhr summed up the mainline Protestant view: "A God without wrath brought men without sin into a kingdom without judgment through the ministrations of a Christ without a cross" (Niebuhr, *The Kingdom of God in America*, 193). Though he wrote this in the 1930s, the same statement could well have been spoken today.

Western society is marked by two dominant forces: (1) an economic system of consumer capitalism, and (2) a political system of liberal democracy. The economic system focuses on meeting the "felt needs" of consumers, and the political system centers on the rights and liberties of individuals. Put together, those forces produce a culture that crowns the individual.

The individual is autonomous and reigns supreme. To question individual rights and choices, values, and "needs" is the height of political incorrectness and must be avoided at all costs.

In such a culture, to talk about sin and the need for salvation is taboo, because sin manifests itself first in the lives and actions of individuals. We seemingly have forgotten Martin Luther's insistence that persons must confront their own sinfulness in all its ravaging depths before they can enjoy the comforts of salvation. Luther took his cue from Paul. No matter where we are on our spiritual journey, we were "once dead." To receive salvation, we must by God's grace recognize our sinfulness and repent. Though we need not be stringently sin conscious, we must always remember who we are: forgiven sinners. Paul gave a powerful reminder of this to his young protégé, Timothy. "This is a true saying, to be completely accepted and believed: Christ Jesus came into the world to save sinners. I am the worst of them, but God was merciful to me in order that Christ Jesus might show his full patience in dealing with me, the worst of sinners, as an example for all those who would later believe in him and receive eternal life" (1 Tim. 1:15-16, GNT).

To forget who we are and who we have been is the doorway to spiritual pride and a roadblock to spiritual growth. The humility that comes through our contrition and repentance opens our hearts to receive the fullness of God's grace—which is to be "made alive in Christ."

REFLECTING AND RECORDING

"A God without wrath brought men without sin into a kingdom without judgment through the ministrations of a Christ without a cross." This statement of Niebuhr is rather scathing. How do you respond to it? How true is this in light of your experience in the church and the preaching and teaching you have experienced?

Tomorrow we will consider the thrilling possibility of being "made alive with Christ." For now let's reflect personally on where we have been and/or where we are in our spiritual journey. The following is Paul's challenge for Christians to walk in newness of life. Read it slowly and contemplatively.

> With the Lord's authority I say this: Live no longer as the Gentiles do, for they are hopelessly confused. Their minds are full of darkness; they wander far from the life God gives because they have closed their minds and hardened their hearts against him. They have no sense of shame. They live for lustful pleasure and eagerly practice every kind of impurity. But that isn't what you learned about Christ. Since you have heard about Jesus and have learned the truth that comes from him, throw off your old sinful nature and your former way of life, which is corrupted by lust and deception. Instead, let the Spirit renew your thoughts and attitudes. Put on your new nature, created to be like God—truly righteous and holy. (Eph. 4:17-24, NLT)

The following phrases appear in the text. Concentrate on each of them as to what degree they may have characterized your life in the past, or in what way they may describe where you are now. Make some notes of your reflections.

"Wander far from the life God gives"

"Closed . . . minds and hardened . . . hearts against [God]"

"Live for lustful pleasure and eagerly practice every kind of impurity"

Offer a prayer of confession and repentance for any of the "old sinful nature" you may feel, and/or a prayer of thanksgiving for having been delivered from "your former way of life."

DURING THE DAY

Were you able to find someone yesterday to talk to about the distinction between following Christ and being in Christ? If not, seek out someone today.

"Being past feeling" is one of the signs of sin in our life. Seek to be sensitive today to your *feelings* as you relate to others, when there is a decision to make that may have moral and ethical implications, and whether there is an occasion when your conscience stirs within.

Continue praying your "invitation to Christ" prayer.

Day 4

POSSIBILITY: MADE ALIVE IN CHRIST

> God, who is rich in mercy, out of the great love with which he loved us even when we were dead through our trespasses, made us alive together with Christ—by grace you have been saved—and raised us up with him and seated us with him in the heavenly places in Christ Jesus, so that in the ages to come he might show the immeasurable riches of his grace in kindness toward us in Christ Jesus. For by grace you have been saved through faith, and this is not your own doing; it is the gift of God—not the result of works, so that no one may boast. For we are what he has made us, created in Christ Jesus for good works, which God prepared beforehand to be our way of life. (Ephesians 2:4-10)

Yesterday we considered the predicament of persons without Christ: they are dead in their trespasses and sins. Paul minced no words in describing the situation.

1. We are controlled by Satan: "You followed the ruler of the kingdom of the air, the spirit who is now at work in those who are disobedient."
2. Apart from Christ, we are pulled to conform to the standards of a world that has no regard for the demands of our God of love, righteousness, peace, and justice, a God who calls us "to be holy as I am holy."
3. When we follow the ways of the world, gratifying the cravings of our sinful nature, we become children of wrath.

This is the scathing reality, and Paul didn't hesitate to present it in stark boldness. Yet, even as the predicament is excruciatingly painful, the possibility is excitingly clear and beckoning: *to be made alive in* Christ.

On Day 5 of last week, we introduced the fact that "in Christ" was a recurring theme for Paul. Two concepts that were important in the apostle's mind have become a part of our understanding of his teaching: (a) In Romans and Galatians, *justification by grace through faith*, and (b) in the majority of his epistles, *a person being in Christ*. These two experiential concepts were a part of the core of Paul's understanding of the Christian experience. In the Protestant Church, we have given far more thought to justification than to the indwelling Christ. Paul makes the radical assertion that the mystery of the ages has now been revealed. That secret is "Christ in you, the hope of glory" (Col. 1:27).

The distilled meaning of these references is that God's mysterious secret that has been hidden "*even from the angels*," which scholars have sought to probe and decipher, has now been revealed. That mystery is Christ, but even more, it is "Christ in you, the hope of glory." Here, then, is the secret, the revelation of the mystery that has been hidden for ages and generations but is now revealed to God's saints: the indwelling Christ—in the believer and in the entire community. The ones left out of the people of God are now brought in—and they share the indwelling Christ together!

The clue to the whole Christian experience, the core of the gospel, is that Christ, by whom and through whom all things were created, who is before all things and in all things, in whom God was pleased for all his fullness to dwell, the firstborn over all creation, the image of the invisible God; this Christ who has primacy over all things, in whom all things hold together, who is the head of the church—this Christ, who will stand at the end of time and be the final judge and triumphal Lord, lives in us, individually and corporately, by the Holy Spirit.

As indicated, this is not a sideline thought of Paul. It is one of two concepts that dominate his writing. I remember when the first glow of this glory began to dawn in my soul. I was a pastor in one of the fastest-growing congregations in Mississippi. I was a "success" in every way ecclesiastical success is measured. I had just graduated from seminary, and this was my first full-time appointment. It was the Cinderella church of the conference. I was the organizing pastor of the congregation, and to see a congregation develop "from scratch" is a unique joy. The membership expanded rapidly; we built beautiful buildings, raised lots of money, and did many exciting things. I was the envy of my colleagues, but in my heart of hearts, I grew weary. There was an unexplainable emptiness. Lives were not being vividly transformed. There was fellowship in the church—but it was not too distinct from the country club. We were highly programmed, and the organization hummed efficiently.

Then the racial crisis in Mississippi in the early 1960s shattered our surface fellowship and pitted friend against friend. I was exhausted, bereft of power other than my own driving commitment for social justice and my desire for "professional success." As is often the case, God intervened through a person. I received an invitation to which I responded and which changed my life. A dear friend, Tom Carruth, invited me to a Christian ashram led by E. Stanley Jones. In my desperate search for deeper meaning and greater impact in my ministry, for energy to struggle through the racial upheaval with integrity of preaching and action, for something more than my own lagging, almost nonexistent spiritual life, I had gathered a few people into a prayer-study group, and a member of the group introduced us to Stanley Jones's then-new book, *In Christ*.

We were just getting into the book when the invitation came to attend the ashram. Though I knew nothing about it, I had read enough of Jones to know he had something I desperately needed. I went to the ashram, and that was the beginning of new life for me, a life consciously *in Christ*. It was not that I was not a Christian. I had been following Christ to the best of my ability. I had received the gift of Jesus' death and resurrection, and I knew I was forgiven and accepted by God. But here was something I had missed—myself as the dwelling place of Christ, the Spirit of the living Lord flowing in me.

I remember vividly the experience at an altar during that ashram week. Brother Stanley asked probingly, as Jesus had thousands of years before, "Do you want to be whole?" (John 5:6). He reiterated what he had been teaching. The possibility of wholeness is in Christ indwelling us.

I longingly and with certainty responded, *"Yes . . . yes!"* I yielded myself more completely than ever before to Christ, inviting him to live his life in me; and I made a new commitment to ministry—a ministry in which I would allow Christ to minister through me.

I have not always lived up to that commitment, but it has been the shaping power of my life. I have discovered that praying is not what it once was—going to God and struggling to discover God's guidance. Rather, prayer is recognizing and cultivating an awareness of Christ's indwelling presence, and seeking to give expression to his presence in my life and work. This does not mean I have not struggled or that my spiritual formation and growth have been consistent and smooth. It does not mean that there has not been suffering, doubt, wrestling, dark nights of the soul, failure in relationship and ministry. All of these, to excruciating depths and degrees, have been my lot. But I can trace a pattern. When I have been intentional in cultivating the awareness of the indwelling Christ, yielded and responsive to that presence, I have known wholeness of life, a vibrancy of spirit and joy, and my ministry has been marked by an obvious spirituality that genuinely blessed others. When I have been slack in that intentional effort of staying alive to his aliveness in me, then my joy diminishes, my confidence deteriorates, what accomplishments I experience seem ponderous and hard-gained, and I discover that no matter how noble my purposes, I am often without power.

This is our glory—can we grasp it?—that at our invitation, responding to our response of faith, Christ enters our lives, becomes a part our beings, indwells us as the empowering and shaping power of our lives.

REFLECTING AND RECORDING

The following is a quote from *In Christ*, the book that impacted my life greatly. This entire workbook journey focuses on abiding in Christ. The following statement is rather radical. Don't engage it by agreeing or disagreeing; simply receive it and spend some time pondering the implications of the claims.

> Being in Christ cannot be a concept, but a condition. It is not a proposition—it is a position. We are actually in Christ. It is a world of its own, with its allegiance, its loyalties, its attitudes, its outlook, its very life. The person who steps into Christ becomes as different from the

ordinary man as the ordinary man is different from the animal. It is not merely a change of location; it is a change of life. (E. Stanley Jones, *In Christ*, 99)

Spend the balance of your time contemplating Paul's description of our predicament: "dead in trespasses and sins," and of our possibility: "made alive in Christ."

DURING THE DAY

Continue praying your "invitation to Christ" prayer three or four times today.

DAY 5

THE HOLY SPIRIT

> After they prayed, the place where they were meeting was shaken. And they were all filled with the Holy Spirit and spoke the word of God boldly. . . . With great power the apostles continued to testify to the resurrection of the Lord Jesus, and much grace was upon them all. (Acts 4:31, 33, NIV)

In our rehearsing the gospel and addressing our predicament and possibility, we have not yet focused on the Holy Spirit. In any consideration of the Christian faith and way, the Holy Spirit cannot and must not be ignored. There could certainly be no adequate consideration of prayer and the dynamic of abiding in Christ apart from the Holy Spirit.

It will always be a mystery, but it is at the heart of our Christian faith: there is one God who eternally exists as three persons: Father, Son, and Holy Spirit. Each person of the Trinity is equal in divine essence. The Holy Spirit is as much God as the Father and the Son. The three—Father, Son, and Holy Spirit—are one in character and action, living and working together in unity. Though always present with the Father and the Son, the Spirit came in a new and powerful way at Pentecost, following the life, ministry, death, and resurrection of Jesus. Jesus had made the promise as he talked about his death: "It is for your good that I am going away. Unless I go away, the Counselor [Holy Spirit] will not come to you; but if I go, I will send him to you" (John 16:7, NIV). After his resurrection and prior to his ascension, Jesus told his followers to stay in Jerusalem until they received the gift promised by him and the Father—the gift of the Holy Spirit, which would provide them the power to be and do all they were called to be and do as his followers.

The book of Acts is the record of the establishment of the church by the Holy Spirit and the ministry of Jesus' followers, empowered by the Spirit. It began dramatically.

> When the day of Pentecost had come, they were all together in one place. And suddenly from heaven there came a sound like the rush of a violent wind, and it filled the entire house where they were sitting. Divided tongues, as of fire, appeared among them, and a tongue rested on each of them. All of them were filled with the Holy Spirit and began to speak in other languages, as the Spirit gave them ability. (2:1-4)

This is the first Pentecost, which happened at the end of a ten-day, round-the-clock prayer meeting, mandated by the risen Lord, who indicated that they were to wait for the gift of the Spirit's outpouring through prayer. The text with which we began describes a kind of second Pentecost, which occurred some time later. It is clear from both incidents that the power and effectiveness of Christ followers and the church as a body is determined by the Spirit's working, and the Spirit's working is connected to the faith and continued prayers of believers. How slow we are in believing that God's giving is inseparably linked with our asking and willingness to receive. After making that phenomenal promise, "Ask and it will be given to you; seek and you will find; knock and the door will be opened" (Luke 11:9, NIV), Jesus made an equally amazing statement: "If you then, who are evil, know how to give good gifts to your children, how much more will the heavenly Father give the Holy Spirit to those who ask him!" (11:13).

Prayer and the Holy Spirit are inseparably linked. The measure of God's gift of the Spirit is connected with our praying. For now, our focused attention is on the Holy Spirit and our abiding in Christ. The primary work of the Holy Spirit is to make Jesus known and provide power by joining us to the risen Christ. Jesus himself made the case. He said that when the Holy Spirit comes, "he will testify about me" (John 15:26, NIV). "He will bring glory to me by taking from what is mine and making it known to you" (John 16:14, NIV).

F. B. Meyer, a renowned New Testament scholar, expressed this primary role of the Holy Spirit in an illuminating way. "[The Holy Spirit] is like a shaft of light that falls on the Beloved Face, so that as in the photograph, you do not think about the light, nor the origin of the light, but you think about the face that it reveals" (quoted in Fred A. Hartley III, *Prayer on Fire*, 46).

The "Beloved Face" is the face of Jesus. The Holy Spirit draws us initially to Christ. The Spirit opens our hearts to Christ and comes to live in us when we receive Christ. The Holy Spirit opens our minds and hearts to see the riches we have in Christ, and softens our hearts to love him more dearly and follow him more nearly.

Simply and sweepingly stated, the work of the Holy Spirit is to provide power by joining us to the risen Christ to abide with him there. By that joining we enter into Christ himself and receive all we need to continue in the Christian life.

In the Old Testament, there are only three places in two contexts that call the Spirit of God the Holy Spirit: Psalm 51:11 and Isaiah 63:10-11. Both these passages refer to God's grief at sin. Apart from these two references, the phrase *Holy Spirit* is absent from the Hebrew canon. Yet, the New Testament contains more than ninety references to the Spirit who makes us holy. The principal mission of Jesus, according to John the Baptist, is to *baptize us in the Holy Spirit*, or immerse us in the character and nature of God himself. The difference between the Old and the New Testaments is the *presence of the Spirit in every believer*. That empowering Presence makes us holy by joining us to the risen Lord. Every believer needs to receive God's empowering presence. Jesus baptizes us into this reality.

Our churches are full of people who believe and affirm some kind of formal faith but are empty and unfulfilled. They lack power and still seek to live by their own resources and strength. Obviously, intellectual assent—belief affirmation—is not enough. *Entering in* the Christian life is more; it is an exercise of the will. The act of putting ourselves—past, present, and future—into God's hands to do with as God pleases is essential.

For a long time I wrestled with Paul's word to the Corinthians, "No one can say 'Jesus is Lord' except by the Holy Spirit" (1 Cor. 12:3). The meaning is clear to me now. To say and mean "Jesus is Lord" is more than intellectual affirmation. It's a decision of the will and a commitment of one's life. We can't do that in our own power. The Holy Spirit moves in our lives when we are open to him, giving us power to come down off the throne of our lives and make Jesus Lord, to enter in the Christian life.

But also, *to continue* in the Christian life.

There are plenty of people who start out in the Christian life full of energy, enthusiasm, and excitement. They're alive and eager. Their whole life is aflame with love and compassion. Their lifestyle is altered. They slough off old habits, change their priorities. They are literally new persons. Then gradually, the fire begins to fade; zeal diminishes. They drift back into old patterns, and before they realize what has happened, they are back to their "old self." The problem? Failure to make themselves available to the power of the Holy Spirit so they can continue in the Christian life.

So we can't talk about the Holy Spirit without considering the language of scripture, the language of "being filled." After "entering in" our life in Christ (conversion, justification by grace through faith, accepting Christ as Savior), the Holy Spirit seeks to saturate our lives completely. God's desire for all of us is "that [we] may be filled to the measure of all the fullness of God"(Eph. 3:19, NIV). The Spirit joins us to the risen Lord and thus joins us to his body, the church, God's new people. There, where we are joined together in who Christ is, we become a home for God's empowering presence, a place in which God dwells by the Spirit

(Eph. 2:22). "For in Christ all the fullness of the Deity lives . . . , and you have been given fullness in Christ" (Col. 2:9, 10). This fullness is given through the Holy Spirit.

REFLECTING AND RECORDING

List the first five words or phrases that come to mind when you think of the Holy Spirit.

Reflect on your faith journey. How much exposure have you had to teaching/preaching on the Holy Spirit? Have you been consciously aware of the Holy Spirit as a factor in your Christian faith? When someone mentions the Holy Spirit or when you think of the Spirit, what churches in your community come to mind?

Spend a few minutes thinking about the role the Holy Spirit has played in your "entering in" and "continuing in" the Christian life.

DURING THE DAY

For the past few days we have been praying a specific prayer, an invitation to Jesus. For the next few days, let's address a prayer to the Holy Spirit. Printed as a cutout on page 203, this prayer is one of the favorite hymns of the church. Pray it now, and put it in a place where it will be available to you to pray three or four times during the day.

> Breathe on me, Breath of God, fill me with life anew,
> that I may love what thou dost love,
> and do what thou wouldst do.
>
> Breathe on me, Breath of God, until my heart is pure,
> until with thee I will one will,
> to do and to endure.
> —Edwin Hatch, "Breathe on Me, Breath of God," in *The United Methodist Hymnal*, no. 420

Day 6

THE NEGLECTED FACTOR

> When they had come together, [the disciples] asked [Jesus], "Lord, is this the time when you will restore the kingdom to Israel?" He replied, "It is not for you to know the times or periods that the Father has set by his own authority. But you will receive power when the Holy Spirit has come upon you; and you will be my witnesses in Jerusalem, in all Judea and Samaria, and to the ends of the earth." (Acts 1:6-8)

One book of the Bible that is least understood by Western mainline Christians, I believe, is the book of Acts, which records the Holy Spirit's work in the lives of those commissioned by Jesus to complete the ministry he began. As they remained *in him*, they would be led by his very own Spirit. Jesus promised, "You will receive power when the Holy Spirit has come upon you." And he told those scared followers to wait in Jerusalem for the promise. They were to live in the promise of his power in praying, and they were to reclaim our fallen world for his Father through being led by his presence. Acts is the account of the dynamic released in the world through men and women of prayer, claiming what Jesus had promised.

Those fearful men and women knew who they were. They knew they couldn't do it in their own power, so they did what Jesus told them to do. They waited. And the scripture says that with one accord, they devoted themselves to prayer. And you know what happened: "Suddenly from heaven there came a sound like the rush of a violent wind, and it filled the entire house where they were sitting."

The way Luke tells the story is thrilling. He stumbles over himself as though grasping for words to describe what happened. And then, he speaks in a restrained way that seems to indicate there's no way to tell about what happened except to put it down in the most simple, straightforward fashion. And so Luke penned one of the most underdramatic sentences in the whole Bible: "All of them were filled with the Holy Spirit." He was as matter-of-fact as that. Something new came into their experience. Out of those closed doors, these formerly timid, frightened men and women went out to proclaim a new gospel—out into the very city that had crucified Jesus, the believers went to boldly tell of his aliveness in the world.

As noted yesterday, the promise is first and foremost the promise of power. And I believe that this is the neglected factor of Pentecost in our lives.

The way I sometimes experience the present-day church causes me to think of the lazy old farmer who lay down beneath a shade tree at lunchtime and said, "You can come or go, breath; I've pulled at you my last time." We lack power. We know little or nothing about the vibrant life described on almost every page of the New Testament. We have given out, and too many of us have given up. We've exhausted our resources. To use a phrase unique to my rural Mississippi culture, we are going on in the Christian life "by main strength and awkwardness."

The New Testament teaches that we were promised fire, not a feeble flicker. We are to be like a city set on a hill, not a smoldering candle hidden under a bushel basket. We are to experience fulfillment for our hunger, the joy and radiance of a wedding feast, excitement like that of a man finding a treasure hidden in the field that leads him to sell everything to possess it.

As Christians, we need to understand that, whether we acknowledge it or not, we are in relationship with the Holy Spirit. Just as we cannot separate the Father and the Son from our Christian life, so we cannot separate ourselves from the Holy Spirit. Recall yesterday's discussion, "No one can say 'Jesus is Lord' except by the Holy Spirit."

Even so, it is clear in scripture and verified in life that we can resist the Holy Spirit. We can even be hostile to the Spirit. Scripture talks specifically about our *grieving* and *quenching* the Holy Spirit.

Ephesians 4:30 warns, "Do not grieve the Holy Spirit." It is clear from the setting of that word that our sins bring sorrow to the Holy Spirit. Extreme anger, lying, deceit, bitterness, lack of forgiveness, and cutting words are the sins specifically mentioned. Think about it. The Holy Spirit attempts to restrain our sinful behavior. The Spirit is a presence and power within, but when we fail to obey him, he grieves.

First Thessalonians 5:19 says, "Quench not the Spirit." That's the wording in the King James and English Revised versions. Other translations render it, "Do not restrain the Holy Spirit" (GNT), "Never try to suppress the Spirit" (JB), "Do not put out the Spirit's fire" (NIV), and "Do not smother the Holy Spirit" (TLB, a paraphrase). The context for this verse lists the activities mobilized by the Holy Spirit: unceasing prayer, continual rejoicing, thanksgiving to God in all circumstances. The Holy Spirit seeks to stir up in our souls the desire to worship, to be passionate intercessors, to demonstrate the joy that is ours as Christ followers. But we resist, we fail to follow the Spirit's lead, and thus we smother the Holy Spirit; we squelch the Spirit's initiative.

So there is active and passive sin in our relationship to the Spirit. We grieve the Holy Spirit by doing what he tells us *not to do*. We quench the Holy Spirit by refusing to do what he tells us *to do*.

Again, we can't talk about the Holy Spirit without considering the language of scripture, the language of "being filled." To be filled with the Spirit is to be saturated with the Spirit. As we will consider tomorrow, since the Holy Spirit and the indwelling Christ are inseparable, to be filled with the Spirit is to abide in Christ, to live in him—letting Christ's love, compassion, truth, kindness, and mercy shape our lives.

REFLECTING AND RECORDING

Whether we acknowledge it or not, we are in relationship with the Holy Spirit. As we cannot separate the Father and the Son from our Christian life, we cannot separate ourselves from the Holy Spirit.

How do you respond to these statements? Are they something you have known, or are they new thoughts? How might your thinking and action change if you stayed aware of these facts?

If you need to, reread the preceding paragraphs about *grieving* and *quenching* the Holy Spirit. The essence is that we grieve the Holy Spirit by doing what he tells us *not to do*, and we quench the Holy Spirit by refusing to do what he tells us *to do*. Make some notes beside each of these categories, indicating how you might have grieved or quenched the Spirit:

grieved

quenched

DURING THE DAY

Continue praying your "Breathe on me, Breath of God" prayer.

DAY 7

THE HOLY SPIRIT AND THE INDWELLING CHRIST

You are not in the flesh; you are in the Spirit, since the Spirit of God dwells in you. Anyone who does not have the Spirit of Christ does not belong to him. But if Christ is in you, though the body is dead because of sin, the Spirit is life because of righteousness. If the Spirit of him who raised Jesus from the dead dwells in you, he who raised Christ from the dead will give life to your mortal bodies also through his Spirit that dwells in you. (Romans 8:9-11)

Christian missionary and theologian E. Stanley Jones observed that the phrase "in Christ" is not found in the three Synoptic Gospels—Matthew, Mark, and Luke. Brother Stanley says the reason for that is obvious: "They were at the stage of Immanuel—'God with us,' but not 'in us.' The account says that Jesus chose twelve 'to be with Him' (Mark 3:14). They were with Him, and not in Him. The 'in Him' stage came after the outpouring of the Holy Spirit at Pentecost. Up to then it was 'with,' and after that, 'in.' The 'with' had to end so that the 'in' might begin. He withdrew His presence and gave them His omnipresence" (*In Christ*, 106).

In John 14, Jesus promised: "I will not leave you orphaned; I am coming to you. . . . and those who love me will be loved by my Father, and I will love them and reveal myself to them" (vv. 18, 21). He then made clear that though he was "going away," he would return and be an abiding presence and the source of life.

Throughout the writings of John and Paul, the phrases "Holy Spirit," "the Spirit of God," and "the Spirit of Christ" are sometimes indistinguishable and appear to be used interchangeably. When Paul speaks of the experience of the believer being led by the Spirit in Romans 8, he speaks of the presence of Christ within by using the following phrases interchangeably: "The Spirit of God," "the Spirit of Christ," and "Christ . . . in you." Perhaps the best way to describe this is that Christ is present to us and within us by his Spirit. In his discourse on the vine and the branches, which followed the John passage referred to above, Jesus provides the foundation for the later understanding of the Spirit of Christ being with us and we in him.

Read again Romans 8:9-11.

Here in this passage, God is present to us and we to him through the indwelling Christ, who abides within us through his Spirit.

> The New Testament makes
> it clear: there is no awareness of the
> presence of the risen Christ to us or
> in us through the Holy Spirit, and there
> can be no convincing validation of
> the claim that one has the Holy Spirit
> unless this is accompanied by signs
> of Jesus' presence.

There are many evidences of God's Spirit. Signs, wonders, acts of power, courage in persecution, anointed preaching, compassionate intercession, and vibrant worship certainly point to the Spirit at work in our midst. But the ultimate sign is that one's life moves toward fullness in Christ, and this always produces deeper faith, hope, and love—*and the greatest of these is love.*

Christ indwells us with his Spirit, and we receive what he promised: power in prayer and the commitment to fulfill his calling to complete his mission—to seek and to save the lost.

You may say it either way: The Holy Spirit is present in us as the indwelling Christ, or Christ is present in us as the Holy Spirit.

James Stewart, a renowned New Testament scholar and preacher, has given a helpful summary response to the question of the identity and distinction of the indwelling Christ and the Spirit in Paul's writings. We cannot help but recognize that the ideas have been blended in a remarkable degree. Continually, in Paul's mind, they are acting and reacting upon each other. Upon the [person] who is united with Christ by faith, the Spirit as a divine gift is bestowed; and the Spirit, in turn, works for the strengthening and intensifying of that union. Only in the light of Christ can the Spirit's true nature be understood; and only by the Spirit's aid can a [person] confess Christ's divinity, and say 'Jesus is Lord' (1 Cor. 12:3)" (Stewart, *A Man in Christ*, quoted in Dunnam, *Alive in Christ*, 49).

So Paul concludes, "If the Spirit of him who raised Jesus from the dead dwells in you, he who raised Christ from the dead will give life to your mortal bodies also through his Spirit that dwells in you" (Rom. 8:11). The Holy Spirit present in us empowers us, joining us to the living Christ, whose priestly life joins us to God forever. There, with him we also "live to intercede." When we are alive in Christ, every part of our life is connected with Christ. We live in Christ (Col. 2:6) and with Christ (Col. 2:13). We are instructed by Christ; his word dwells in us (Col. 3:16). Our relationship with Christ shapes our relationship with others. Christ within us forms the atmosphere in which we live. To the degree that we are yielded to the Holy Spirit as the indwelling Christ, we manifest Christ's presence in the world. This is an extravagant and powerful possibility, the meaning of which we will pursue in the coming days.

REFLECTING AND RECORDING

In the space provided to the right of the statement on page 55, rewrite the statement to express in your own words the connection between the risen Christ and the Holy Spirit.

Thumb through the days of this week, reviewing the content. What new insights did you have? What issues brought the most questions? How were you challenged? Did you disagree with something? What meant the most to you? Make some notes here.

If you are in a group studying this workbook, think of the members of your group and of your gathering together. Do you know of specific needs of any of those persons? Pray for them. Commit yourself to listen, to hear, to share honestly and openly, claiming that you have a contribution to make.

DURING THE DAY

Continue praying your "Breathe on Me, Breath of God" prayer.

GROUP MEETING FOR WEEK TWO

INTRODUCTION

Participation in a group like the one studying this book involves a covenant relationship. You will profit most from daily use of this workbook if you faithfully attend weekly meetings. Don't feel guilty if you have to miss a day in the workbook. Don't hesitate to share any difficulty you have with the group. We learn something about ourselves when we share our thoughts and feelings with others. You may discover, for instance, that you are subconsciously afraid of dealing with the content of a particular day because its requirements might reveal something about you. Be patient with yourself and always remain open to what God may be seeking to teach you.

Your spiritual growth, in part, hinges upon your group participation, so share as openly as you can and listen to what others say. If you are attentive, you may pick up meaning beyond the surface of their words. Participating sensitively in this fashion is crucial. Responding immediately to the feelings you discern is also important. At times the group may need to focus its entire attention upon a particular individual. If some need or concern is expressed, the leader may ask the group to enter into a brief period of special prayer. But participants should not depend solely upon the leader for this kind of sensitivity. Even if you aren't the leader, don't hesitate to ask the group to join you in special prayer. This praying may be silent, or someone may wish to lead the group in a verbal prayer.

Remember that *you* have a contribution to make to the group. Even if you consider your thoughts or experiences trivial or unimportant, they may be exactly what another person needs to hear. Don't seek to be profound but simply to share your experience. Also, if you happen to say something that is not well received or is misunderstood, don't be defensive or critical of yourself or others. Don't get diverted by overly scrutinizing your words and actions. Saint Francis de Sales said, "It is self-love which makes us anxious to know whether what we have said or done is approved or not" (*A Year with the Saints*, 209).

SHARING TOGETHER

Leader: Time may not permit you to use all the suggestions each week. Select what will most benefit your group. Be thoroughly familiar with these suggestions so that you can move through them selectively according to the direction in which the group is moving and according to the time available. Plan ahead, but do not hesitate to change your plans in response to the sharing taking place and the needs that emerge.

1. Open your time together with the leader offering a brief prayer of thanksgiving for the opportunity of sharing with the group, and petitions for openness in sharing and loving responses to one another.
2. If concerns for discussion arose at the close of your last meeting that you were unable to address, take some time to do that.
3. Go to the Reflecting and Recording section of Day 1. Spend eight to ten minutes discussing the responses individuals made to the two reflection statements.
4. Invite a couple of persons to volunteer to share their response, on Day 2, to the difference between *following Christ* and *being in Christ*. Spend some time discussing this idea. Be sure to pay attention in your discussion to the possibilities of being "dead in trespasses and sins" and being "made alive in Christ."
5. Invite someone to read the last four paragraphs of Day 6; then spend as much time as needed discussing how we *grieve* and *quench* the Holy Spirit. Encourage persons to share specific experiences.
6. Invite two or three people to read how they rewrote the paragraph about the risen Christ and the Holy Spirit in their Reflecting and Recording time, Day 7.
7. Spend the balance of your time discussing any issue that someone may be interested in that you have not yet covered.

PRAYING TOGETHER

1. Praying corporately each week is a special ministry. Invite individuals to mention any special needs or concerns they wish to share with the entire group. A good pattern may be to ask for a period of prayer after each need is mentioned. This may be silent prayer, or one person may offer a brief two- or three-sentence verbal prayer.
2. Close your time by praying together the Lord's Prayer.

ALIVE IN CHRIST

Day 1

INVITATION: COME UNTO ME

> Come to me, all you who are weary and burdened, and I will give you rest. Take my yoke upon you and learn from me, for I am gentle and humble in heart, and you will find rest for your souls. For my yoke is easy and my burden is light." (Matthew 11:28-30, NIV)

This Gospel passage is one of the most familiar in the Bible. Perhaps you memorized verse 28 from the King James Version: "Come unto me, all ye that labor and are heavy laden, and I will give you rest." For centuries this passage has been used to comfort those in grief, to encourage those who are struggling, and to give hope to those who are in despair. We know it and recall it in tough times, trusting the One who has extended the invitation.

"Come unto me" is a wonderful invitation from our Lord himself. It's not only an invitation but also a promise: "You will find rest for your souls. For my yoke is easy."

Because the invitation and promise are such a source of strength and encouragement, most of us have probably not noted the setting of this word of Jesus in Matthew's Gospel. This can be a problem. If we do not know the setting, we may misunderstand and misappropriate the meaning or even miss a dimension of profound meaning.

Clearly, Jesus does not mean that in this life all our weariness and burdens of work, poor health, poverty, and the like will disappear. It is true that one day all our burdens will be lifted, but that will happen in God's eternal future, not in the here and now. Jesus is speaking to his followers in the midst of their participation in his mission. "Come to me **now** and I will give you rest **now**. Take my yoke upon you." What is this rest? What is this "yoke" that we are to take upon ourselves, a yoke that is easy? The setting will help us with an answer to these questions.

Reading the earlier part of Matthew 11, we realize that Jesus himself is disappointed and angry. Even John the Baptist seems not to have understood what was happening. Verse 20 adds to the picture. "Then Jesus began to denounce the cities in which most of his miracles had been performed, because they did not repent" (NIV). If he didn't scream, he certainly forcefully said, "Woe to you." The Israelite cities were refusing his deeds and his message, while if such deeds had been done in pagan cities (even in Sodom!) they would have repented, Jesus said.

In his disappointment and rage, what did Jesus do? He prayed. Not as you and I would probably pray. We would rant and call upon God to judge. There would probably be some questioning of why God doesn't intervene, and certainly there would be some self-pity—"Why do I have to take all this?" But not Jesus. He offered a prayer of thanks and praise. "I praise you, Father, Lord of heaven and earth, because you have hidden these things from the wise and learned and revealed them to little children" (11:25, NIV). Amazingly, Jesus was disappointed and angry, but he was not discouraged by an unresponsive world, because he trusted in the Father's sovereignty over all creation. He knew that "this was [the Father's] good pleasure" (v. 26, NIV).

What are "these things" that are hidden from the wise, and what is it that is God's will? Jesus is talking about God's radical focusing of the divine word and work in his person and ministry. He states it in verse 27: "All things have been committed to me by my Father. No one knows the Son except the Father, and no one knows the Father except the Son and those to whom the Son chooses to reveal him" (NIV).

Here is a radical assertion and a fundamental Christian truth. Despite all the knowledge of God claimed by people of all ages and religions, no one really knows the Father except Jesus, the Son, and those to whom the Son reveals him. Such is the Father's gracious will. It is at this point, with the whole reality and power and being of God concentrated in Jesus, that Jesus speaks the familiar words, "Come to me . . . and I will give you rest." He is not talking about rest as we normally perceive it, nor is he referring to some eternal rest far off in the future. He is speaking of our being connected to God, finding that rest to which Saint Augustine alluded when he said that our hearts are forever restless until we find rest in God. We find our rest in God when we come to Jesus.

We find everything there is to know of God in Jesus. Not in Christianity or the church, not in doctrine or dogma. Not even in the Bible. To be sure, it is likely that we have found Jesus through Christianity, through the church, in the Bible. But these are instruments God uses to reach us. Sometimes, however, they may be obstacles, things that get between us and God. So Jesus invites us, "Come unto me."

It is to us who have heard this call "Come unto me" that there is a second equally loving and compelling invitation: "Abide in me." We will begin to look intently at this second invitation tomorrow. For now, think of coming to Jesus in the terms he used: "Take my yoke upon you, and learn from me; for I am gentle and humble in heart, and you will find rest for your souls. For my yoke is easy, and my burden is light" (vv. 29-30).

Most of us know little about yokes, so to take a yoke upon ourselves, even the yoke of Christ, does not sound very appealing. It may help if we see a picture of a yoke as it used to be in the days of Jesus, a time when a yoke was as much a necessity as food and drink because it was essential in the labor that provided the food and drink that meant survival.

One of the wonderful legends handed down about the mysterious, quiet years of Jesus is that Jesus the carpenter was one of the master yoke makers in the Nazareth area. People came from miles around for a yoke that was hand-carved and crafted by Jesus, the son of Joseph. Perhaps as Jesus extended his invitation "Come unto me, . . . For my yoke is easy, and my burden is light," he thought of a customer driving a team of oxen into his courtyard. As a yoke maker, Jesus probably spent considerable time studying the oxen, measuring their height, their necks and shoulders, and the space between them. Within a week, the team would be brought back, and Jesus would carefully place the newly made yoke over the oxen's shoulders, examining how well it fit, careful about rough places, smoothing out the edges, and fitting them perfectly to this particular team of oxen.

That's the kind of yoke Jesus invites us to take. Do not be misled by the word *easy*. The root word in Greek speaks directly of the tailor-made yokes: they were "well-fitting." The yoke Jesus invites us to take, the yoke that in itself brings rest to weary souls, is one that is made exactly to fit our lives and hearts. The yoke he invites us to wear fits us well. His yokes were usually designed for two oxen. Our yoke is for two, and our yoke partner is none other than Christ himself.

REFLECTING AND RECORDING

Spend three or four minutes reflecting on how Christianity, the church, and the Bible have been instruments God has used to reach you for Christ—or how they have been obstacles.

Recall an occasion when Jesus' invitation, "Come unto me," meant most to you. Write a few sentences to get that experience clearly in mind.

What connection do you make between Jesus' promise of rest and his invitation, "Take my yoke upon you"?

DURING THE DAY

Off and on for many years, my morning ritual has included a word to myself. Sometimes I speak it aloud; sometimes I simply think about it. At times I have turned it into a kind of mantra, repeating it as I breathe in and out. *"Maxie, the secret is simply this: 'Christ in you! Yes,*

Christ in you; bringing with him the hope of all the glorious things to come.'" * That's J. B. Phillips' translation of Colossians 1:27 addressed to me personally. This text is printed on page 203 with space for you to write your name. Cut it out and keep it with you during the coming days. Say the word aloud to yourself every morning; try to find other times to repeat it during the day.

Day 2

INVITATION: ABIDE IN ME

> Abide in me as I abide in you. Just as the branch cannot bear fruit by itself unless it abides in the vine, neither can you unless you abide in me. (John 15:4)

Yesterday we considered that gracious, welcoming invitation of Jesus, "Come unto me, all ye that labor and are heavy laden, and I will give you rest" (Matt. 11:28, KJV). It's one of those heart-known verses of scripture that has been a touchstone in the lives of so many. In this verse and the following one, Jesus offers rest. As suggested yesterday, he is not talking about rest as we normally perceive it, nor is he referring to some eternal rest far in the future. He is speaking of our being connected to God, finding the rest that is ours only in God when we come to Jesus.

Stating the offer of rest twice begs for more attention. Andrew Murray guides us to think clearly about the offer.

> First the Savior said, *"Come unto me . . . and I will give you rest"*; the . . . moment you come, and believe, I will give you rest. . . . All that God bestows needs time to become fully our own. . . . And so the Savior repeats His promise, in words that clearly speak . . . of the deeper and personally appropriated rest of the soul that abides with Him. He now not only said, *"Come unto me,"* but *"Take my yoke upon you and learn of me"*: become my scholars, yield yourselves to my training, submit in all things to my will, let your whole life be one with Mine—in other words, abide in Me." (*Andrew Murray on Prayer*, 21–22)

So, the extended invitation is to abide. It is not simply an invitation to "come unto me," or even to "come, follow me." It is an invitation to "come and stay" with Christ. The Greek root word, *meno*, from which we derive the term *abide* is prevalent in scripture. Quite often it is used in an ordinary way to signify that someone remained or stayed in a certain place. There is also the more profound "abiding" in the sense of deep togetherness, bonding, and deeper yet, *union*. Even in these unordinary instances, the New International Version uses the word *remain* as the primary translation for *meno* (abide).

The day when he baptized Jesus, John the Baptist bore this witness: "I saw the Spirit come down from heaven as a dove and *remain* on him" (John 1:32, NIV, emphasis added). The NIV also uses the word *remain* in Jesus' invitation connected with the vine and branches metaphor. "Remain in me, and I will remain in you. No branch can bear fruit by itself; it must remain in the vine. Neither can you bear fruit unless you remain in me" (John 15:4). Later in this same chapter, John records Jesus' invitation about "abiding" in his love, and again the NIV uses the word *remain*. "As the Father has loved me, so have I loved you. Now remain in my love" (v. 9).

The invitation is not only to come, not only to follow, but to "come and stay."

REFLECTING AND RECORDING

Read again the paragraph from Andrew Murray.

Murray tells us that the rest Jesus provides is the rest of pardon, acceptance, and love. Make some notes about the nature of this *rest* as you have received it.

The rest of pardon

The rest of acceptance

The rest of Jesus' love for me

How has the *rest* Jesus offers expressed itself in other ways in your life?

"Take my yoke upon you, and learn of me" is the other dimension of this invitation of Jesus. Read again the last sentence of Murray's statement, and spend some time reflecting on how you have responded, or how you need to respond, to this invitation.

DURING THE DAY

Continue speaking "The secret is simply this" word to yourself.

DAY 3

IN CHRIST

> I myself have been made a minister of the same gospel, and though it is true at this moment that I am suffering on behalf of you who have heard the gospel, yet I am far from sorry about it. Indeed, I am glad, because it gives me a chance to complete in my own sufferings something of the untold pains which Christ suffers on behalf of his body, the Church. For I am a minister of the Church by divine commission, a commission granted to me for your benefit and for a special purpose: that I might fully declare God's Word—that sacred mystery which up till now has been hidden in every age and every generation, but which is now as clear as daylight to those who love God. They are those to whom God has planned to give a vision of the full wonder and splendor of his secret plan for the nations. And the secret is simply this: Christ in you! Yes, Christ in you bringing with him the hope of all the glorious things to come. (Colossians 1:23b-27, Phillips*)

As we saw in Week 1, some of the most vivid and important reflections on the person and work of Christ are found in Colossians. Paul makes it clear that God's great purposes for individuals and for the world is focused in Christ. What has been a mystery is no longer a mystery. The secret is out! God's purpose of Christ indwelling everyone has now been revealed.

"In Christ" was a recurring theme for Paul. As indicated earlier, a huge part of his understanding of the Christian life revolved around two basic concepts: (1) justification by grace through faith, and (2) a *person in Christ*. These two experiential concepts are the springs from which all other expressions and experiences of the Christian life flow.

It interests me that in all his letter writing, Paul did not describe his Damascus road experience. (He alluded to it in Galatians 1:3-17, especially verse 16.) Luke records that dramatic testimony in the Acts of the Apostles, which describes how Paul was struck down by a blinding light and heard the voice of Christ. But in his letters, rather than describing the event, Paul talked about its meaning. That meaning was deepened as he reflected and prayed in the Arabian desert before he began to preach the message to all who would listen.

In many instances he virtually sings about it, such as in his word to the Colossians: "God has planned to give a vision of the full wonder and splendor of his secret plan for the nations. And the secret is simply this: Christ *in you*! Yes, Christ *in you* bringing with him the hope of all the glorious things to come."

What a breathtaking possibility—unbelievable apart from faith—that we can live our lives *in Christ*. It is an extravagant claim and could be passed off without much attention if this were an isolated instance, but not so. "In Christ," "in union with Christ," and "Christ in you" are recurring words in Paul's vocabulary. Variations of that phrase occur no fewer than 172 times in the New Testament. Paul's definition of a Christian is a person *in Christ*. "If anyone is *in Christ*, there is a new creation: everything old has passed away; see, everything has become new!" (2 Cor. 5:17, emphasis added).

When John Wesley translated this bold affirmation of Paul, he adhered to the original Greek text: "If *anyone* be in Christ, *there* is a new creation." He then added, "Only the power that makes a world can make a Christian." Paul would agree with that. In fact, he gives testimony to it in his two-sentence autobiography: "I have been crucified with Christ; and it is no longer I who live, but it is Christ who lives in me. And the life I now live in the flesh I live by faith in the Son of God, who loved me and gave himself for me" (Gal. 2:19-20).

Paul's two great concepts—justification by grace through faith and Christ indwelling us—are brought together in Paul himself: crucified with Christ, alive in him.

Protestant Christians have championed justification by grace through faith, but we have been slow in claiming the glorious possibility of being alive in Christ, living in the confidence that the presence of God in Jesus Christ is not to be experienced only on occasion, but the indwelling Christ is to become the shaping power of our lives.

Certainly we must not diminish the foundation of our Christian experience—that we are justified by grace through faith. That is the reason we spent the first week of our workbook journey rehearsing the gospel, emphasizing our salvation by grace through faith in the life, death, and resurrection of Jesus. What is glaringly missing is the conviction and confidence that we can live our lives, daily, *in Christ*, and reflect his likeness to the world. This is not an individual experience alone, but the experience of the whole church, as separated people (Jew and Gentile in New Testament days) are brought together into one new body with Christ as the head.

REFLECTING AND RECORDING

Look back at your Christian journey. Below is a time line for your life. Beginning at the left, designate whatever time in your life you began to be conscious of religious questions, yearnings, growth, struggle. Let the right end designate the present. Move through your life and designate specific experiences or periods of time when you were keenly aware of something of a spiritual nature taking place. Occasions such as baptism, confirmation, conversion, vocational decisions, particular commitments, church involvements may be pegs upon which to hang your reflections. Number these in sequence on the time line (1, 2, 3, etc.).

Spiritual Growth Begins <————————————————————> Present

Now write a brief word about each of these experiences or periods of time in the numbered spaces. If more than five, use the extra space.

1.

2.

3.

4.

5.

Could any one of these experiences be described as your "justification by grace through faith" experience?

If there is not a single experience of "justification" on your time line, how would you explain or interpret that fact in your life?

We will be considering this all week long, but spend the balance of your time thinking about my claim that Protestant Christianity has been slow in claiming, along with justification by grace through faith, the glorious possibility of being alive in Christ.

DURING THE DAY

John Wesley named *conferencing* as one of the primary disciplines for spiritual growth. He meant by this the kind of experience we are suggesting if you are using this workbook as a group endeavor. I believe it can be reduced to a simple expression: two or three people intentionally sharing how they are "getting on" in their Christian walk. So in the last two weeks as a "during the day" exercise, I suggested that you find someone with whom to share an idea that we are dealing with in this workbook journey. Now we have a name for it—*Christian conferencing.*

Find someone today with whom you can begin a conversation something like this: "I'm studying a book about prayer and abiding in Christ. The writer says that the apostle Paul put as much emphasis on *being in Christ* as he did on *justification by grace through faith.* We are just getting into the meaning of *being in Christ*, and I don't know too much about it, but I wonder what you think about this."

Continue speaking to yourself "The secret is simply this" word.

Day 4

IMPARTATION OF LIFE

> I am the true vine, and My Father is the vinedresser. Every branch in Me that does not bear fruit He takes away; and every branch that bears fruit He prunes, that it may bear more fruit. You are already clean because of the word which I have spoken to you. Abide in Me, and I in you. As the branch cannot bear fruit of itself, unless it abides in the vine, neither can you, unless you abide in Me. I am the vine, you are the branches. He who abides in Me, and I in him, bears much fruit; for without Me you can do nothing. (John 15:1-5)

Paul's use of the terms "in Christ," "in union with Christ," and having "Christ in you" pervades his writing. Unmistakably, this is his understanding of the Christian faith and life.

But it is not only Paul who uses that language. In the above passage, Jesus uses the metaphor of the vine and the branches. Using this language, he tells us who God is: "My Father is the vinedresser." Then he tells us who he is: "I am the vine." He completes the metaphor by telling us who we are in relation to him: "I am the vine, you are the branches. He who abides in Me, and I in him, bears much fruit; for without Me you can do nothing."

Jesus came to bring himself to us and, in bringing himself, to bring God. He justifies us by providing full pardon for our sin; not only so, he indwells us to give us the power to be and do everything God requires us to be and do. One understanding of redemption is the "impartation of life." Jesus said, "I am come that [you] might have life, and that [you] might have it more abundantly" (John 10:10*b*, KJV). God's gift to us is a new kind of life—the life of Christ himself. The incarnation continues as Christ lives on in us. This is the amazing promise of Jesus: "Abide in Me, and I in you."

Julian "Hule" Goddard, coordinator of the outdoor leadership minor program in youth ministry at Columbia International University in South Carolina, is a unique and trusted friend. His simple, forthright, uncomplicated Christian witness is contagious. He tells the story of preaching a sermon on this invitation of Jesus to "abide me as I abide in you." He elaborated on Jesus identifying himself as the vine and us as the branches. He put it like this: "Jesus is the Vine, and we are the branches. We are like the branch, whose primary task is to suck the sap out of the vine. That makes us sapsuckers." He was rather proud of that aphorism that I grew up hearing and using in rural Mississippi—"sapsuckers."

After the sermon, a PhD botany student engaged him in response to the sermon. While she had profited from the sermon, she gently reminded Hule that he had gotten the part about the vine and the branches wrong. She explained that the way the vine and branches work is a process something like homeostasis—the branches do not suck the sap out of the vine; rather, the vine literally forces its substance in the branches. The task of the branch is not to labor, sucking for the sap, but to "abide" in the vine, open to what the vine provides, the very sap of life and fruitfulness.

As we considered on Days 1 and 2 of this week, Jesus' invitation is a dual one: "Come unto me" and "abide in me." Notice that he did not say, "Come to me and abide *with* me," but "abide *in* me."

As we abide in Christ, every part of our life becomes connected to him. The Vine (Jesus) and the branches (us) share a common life. The life of the Vine becomes the life of the branches. We learn to say yes to Christ every day. I doubt that a time will come in our lives when we will not need to change—when some aspect of our being, newly discovered, will not need Christ's redeeming power. I doubt whether the time will ever come—though I pray for it for myself—when we can say with all confidence and certainty: "I'm yours, Lord. Everything about me, and all of me, is yours." For even when we pray that prayer, revelation comes, and a hidden area or a concern emerges to awareness, and we have to make another commitment and yield ourselves to transforming love.

As we abide in him, we share not only his intentions and purposes but also his life. Amazingly and mysteriously, we live by the life of Christ to the point that we can say with Paul, "It is no longer I who live, but it is Christ who lives in me" (Gal. 2:20).

REFLECTING AND RECORDING

Spend a few minutes reflecting on the claim that Christ came to bring himself to us, and in bringing himself, to bring God. Not only does he justify us by providing full pardon for our sin, but also he indwells us to give us the power to be and do all those things God requires us to be and do.

Have you noted the pervasive "in Christ" language in Paul's writing? Being in Christ, abiding in Christ. Is this news for you? Have you heard it before? Ask yourself this question: What, if anything, in my life reflects the presence and power of the indwelling Christ? Make some notes here.

Return to the time line of your religious journey, which you recorded yesterday. Is there anything there that might suggest or even hint at an awareness of, or a need for, the ongoing presence of Christ in your life?

DURING THE DAY

Did you find anyone to conference with yesterday? How did it go? If not, find someone today. You should have more to add to the conversation.

We've indicated that memory is a precious gift of God, and memorizing is a powerful tool for spiritual growth. We have also suggested that hymns are a great resource for reflection and meditation. The last stanza of one of Charles Wesley's greatest hymns, "And Can It Be That I Should Gain," is printed on page 203. Cut it out and carry it with you, with the goal of having memorized it in three or four days.

Day 5

A LIFE HIDDEN WITH CHRIST IN GOD

> Since, then, you have been raised with Christ, set your hearts on things above, where Christ is seated at the right hand of God. Set your minds on things above, not on earthly things. For you died, and your life is now hidden with Christ in God. When Christ, who is your life, appears, then you also will appear with him in glory. (Colossians 3:1-4, NIV)

I had never heard the term until recently: *ideaviruses*. I don't know how long the word has been around. Seth Godin, a marketing guru, coined it. He uses the word to articulate metabolic growth in relation to marketing and ideas in general.

Michael Frost and Alan Hirsch, who introduced me to the word, describe it in this fashion: "An ideavirus is a big idea that runs amok across the target audience. It's a fashionable idea that captures the thinking and imagination of a section of the population, reaching and changing and influencing everyone it touches. . . . An ideavirus is simply an idea that becomes contagious in precisely the same way that a virus does" (Frost and Hirsch, *The Shaping of Things to Come*, 214).

Godin asserts "that in our rapidly, instantly changing world, the art and science of building, launching, and profiting from ideaviruses is the next frontier. I need to think more about that, but I believe he is right.

What we have been discussing the past few days was an idea that Paul hoped would become an ideavirus. He articulated it every way he could, and in Colossians 3:3 boiled it down to this: "For you died, and your life is now hidden with Christ in God" (NIV). In my book *Alive in Christ*, I shared an experience that made this idea of Paul come alive like a virus in me.

This experience was my friendship with a Benedictine monk. The way we live out our lives is vastly different, but I felt a real kinship, a oneness of spirit with Brother Sam. One of my most memorable evenings, one to which I return often in my mind, is the time he and I spent together alone in my home in Nashville, sharing our Christian pilgrimages. The vivid highlight of that evening was his sharing with me the occasion of his solemn vows, the service when he made his life commitment to the Benedictine community and the monastic life. The vow involved a marked separation from the world to live in poverty, chastity, and obedience.

Brother Sam said that on that day, he prostrated himself before the altar of the chapel, facedown in the very place where his coffin will sit when he dies. As he was lying there, he was covered with a funeral pall, and the death bell began to toll, the bell that rings at the earthly parting of a brother, and it sounded the solemn tones of death. Then there was silence, the deep silence of death. That silence was broken by the singing of the Colossians word, "For you died, and your life is now hidden with Christ in God." After that powerful word, there was more silence as Brother Sam reflected upon his solemn vow. Then the community broke into singing Psalm 118, which is always a part of the Easter liturgy in the Benedictine community. Verse 17 of that psalm says, "I shall not die, but live, and declare the works of the LORD."

After this resurrection proclamation, the liturgist shouted a verse from Ephesians, "Awake, you who sleep; Arise from the dead, and Christ will give you light" (5:14, NKJV). Then the bells of the abbey began to ring joyfully. Brother Sam rose, the funeral pall fell off, the white robe of the Benedictine order was placed upon him, he received the kiss of peace from all of his brothers, and was welcomed into that community to live a life "hidden with Christ in God."

It was a great liturgy of death and resurrection and a symbolic reenactment of the Christian experience. When Brother Sam and I shared, I relived in vivid memory my own baptism, in a rather cold creek in rural Mississippi, in September. Paul gave powerful witness to the idea. Baptism is a vivid expression of the Christian life: a life "hidden with Christ in God." It is that image we are pursuing in this workbook. The image abounds, especially in Colossians and Ephesians.

"You have been given fullness in Christ" (Col. 2:10, NIV).

"Having been buried with him in baptism and raised with him through your faith in the power of God" (Col. 2:12).

"Even when we were dead through our trespasses, [God] made us alive together with Christ" (Eph. 2:5).

C. S. Lewis states the case with unmistakable clarity: "The Church exists for nothing else but to draw [people] into Christ, to make them little Christs. If they are not doing that, all the cathedrals, clergy, missions, sermons, even the Bible itself, are simply a waste of time" (Lewis, *Mere Christianity*, 169–70).

This is a breathtaking truth. To claim it and make it real is our role in the drama of creation and redemption. We become one with Christ, thus becoming "little Christs." We will explore this idea more fully in the days ahead. For now focus on the following: there is always a distinction between the vine and the branches. The branches do not sustain the vine; the vine sustains the branches. But claim this exhilarating truth: the vine cannot express itself except through the branches. Christ is dependent upon us for the expression of his life in the world.

REFLECTING AND RECORDING

In the hymn you are memorizing, Charles Wesley connects "justification" and being "in Christ." "No condemnation now I dread" (justification), "Jesus, and all in him, is mine" (grace); "alive in him, my living Head, and clothed in righteousness divine" (being in Christ). Reflect on the wedding of these two dynamics and to what degree they are present in your life.

Read again the statement of C. S. Lewis. How do you feel about Lewis's statement—is it true? too strong? What about his contention that we are to be "little Christs"?

Spend the balance of your time thinking about the implication for you personally, and for the Christian community of which you are a part, of the statement: *Christ is dependent upon us for the expression of his life in the world.*

DURING THE DAY

Continue your effort to memorize Wesley's hymn.

As you move through the day, seek to find occasions where Christ may be dependent upon you for the expression of his life in the world.

DAY 6

WALK WORTHY OF YOUR CALLING

I therefore, the prisoner in the Lord, beg you to lead a life worthy of the calling to which you have been called, with all humility and gentleness, with patience, bearing with one another in love, making every effort to maintain the unity of the Spirit in the bond of peace. There is one body and one Spirit, just as you were called to the one hope of your calling, one Lord, one faith, one baptism, one God and Father of all, who is above all and through all and in all. (Ephesians 4: 1-6)

When my city, Memphis, is mentioned almost anywhere in the world, people think of Elvis Presley, Beale Street, or barbecue—the best barbecue in the world. You may argue about the barbecue, but not about the music, not about Elvis and Beale Street and the birth of the blues.

You probably are familiar with Elvis, and you have heard of Beale Street. But have you heard of B. B. King? A patriarch of Beale Street, he is one of the most influential blues players of all time. B. B. was present (Sept. 13–14, 2008) when his hometown (Indianola, Mississippi) opened the B. B. King Museum in connection with King's eighty-third birthday (September 16). When he saw his name on the front of the museum, he said, "My goodness, I didn't go to school long enough to be able to tell you how I feel. But I have heard that heaven is beautiful. If heaven is more beautiful than the way I feel today, I'm ready to go tomorrow."

B. B. King almost became a preacher. He became interested in the guitar at age six while watching the Reverend Archie Fair play and sing at the Sanctified Church of God in Christ in Indianola. When people express amazement at King's playing, the lightning-quick movement of his fingers, he simply says his fingers are an extension of his soul.

That's the point of this little excursion into the culture of blues music. Ponder it. His fingers, producing the indescribable music that has made him world-renowned—his fingers, *an extension of his soul.* King even connected the word about his fingers with his expertise in picking cotton as a teenager. He knew he was good. He could pick more than 400 pounds of cotton a day; his personal best was 480 pounds.

Picking cotton, playing the guitar, fingers—*an extension of the soul.* Paul spoke with that kind of gravitas: one of his favorite metaphors for the Christian life is walking. He uses it over and over again, especially in his Ephesians letter. *"Walk worthy of [your] calling* (4:1, NKJV); *"walk in love* (5:2, NIV); *"walk as children of light"* (5:8); *"walk . . . , not as fools but as wise"* (5:15).

We focus today on the first: *"Walk worthy of [your] calling."* I like the King James Version rendering better. "Walk worthy of [your] *vocation.*" Vocation has a more permanent ring to it. Our "calling" is not for a season, something we hear today that may fade or grow faint tomorrow. Two words, "laity" (*laos*) and "*apostolate,*" which we use in the Christian church, add meaning to our calling. Christians are the *laos*, the laity, "the whole people of God," and are a part of the *apostolate*, those to whom the ministry of Christ is committed. Our lives are to be a vocation for Christ, and we should constantly ask, "What apostolic action today will reflect my vocation?"

You may have noticed our opening scripture began with the word *therefore.* That humble word, a mere adverb and conjunction, has significant meaning.

Paul has told the story of grace, the drama of salvation, and now can say "therefore." It is after we know that "by grace [we] have been saved" (2:5) that we can "walk worthy of [our] calling." It is out of his love that we can walk in love. Because he has delivered us from darkness, we "walk as children of light." He has saved us from the devices of our own futile and finite minds, therefore, we can walk "not as fools but as wise."

The source of our calling, of our vocation, is clear. It is Christ himself. Don't let this slip by you. Paul literally sang about it. He begins in chapter 1 singing about the riches of God's grace. He calls God "the Father of all glory."

The crowning wonder is that these riches and glory are our inheritance. In Ephesians 1:6, Paul put it this way: "To the praise of his glorious grace that he freely bestowed on us in the Beloved," that is, *in Christ*. God has given us the riches of his grace in Christ Jesus. And he is the source of our calling, the source of our vocation. Praise belongs to him, and our lives are to be the doxology. Paul calls us to walk worthy of our vocation, then immediately records the signs that reflect the "worthiness" of our vocation.

Does it surprise you that he begins with humility? "With all lowliness" is how the King James Version renders it. Greek New Testament scholars note that the word translated here as lowliness (*tapeinophrosune*) was actually coined by the Christian faith and means humility. In the Greek world there was no word that could communicate what Christians knew was a sure "sign" of their vocation. The Greek adjective from which this uniquely Christian word was compounded always connoted cringing servility, cowering slavishness.

The King James Version lists meekness as the second distinct "sign" of our walking worthy of our vocation. Most new translations connect them in a narrative description. They are twins: humility and meekness. Together or apart, these distinct signs of our Christian walk have nothing to do with weakness. They indicate a strength that knows who it is and a submission to others for the sake of Christ.

The cross and the basin and towel are symbols of humility and meekness. The cross symbolizes submission; the basin and towel, service. Bernard of Clairvaux said, "Learn the lesson that, if you are to do the work of a prophet, what you need is not a scepter but a hoe" (quoted in Foster, *Celebration of Discipline*, 126). Prophets are humble and meek. They know who they are—submissive servants for Christ's sake.

The argument that arose among the disciples in the upper room at the Last Supper was over which of them was the greatest. Isn't it true that most of the time when there is trouble over who is the greatest, there is trouble over who is the least? Most of us know that we will not be the greatest, but we do not want to be the least.

Isn't that also the problem in families, in the workplace, in our congregations? But mark it down. Humility and meekness produce a willingness to be least if obedience to God requires it.

The *source* of our calling is Christ himself: we act out of response to his loving action toward us. The *signs* of our vocation are humility, meekness, longsuffering, love, and peace. We live worthy of our vocation only as we abide in Christ.

REFLECTING AND RECORDING

In light of today's focus, read the following contemporary scriptural expression of the signs of our walking worthy of our calling.

> In light of all this, here's what I want you to do. While I'm locked up here, a prisoner for the Master, I want you to get out there and walk—better yet, run—on the road God called

> you to travel. I don't want you sitting around on your hands. I don't want anyone strolling off down some path that goes nowhere. And mark that you do this with humility and discipline—not in fits and starts, but steadily, putting yourselves out for each other in acts of love, alert at noticing differences and quick at mending fences. (Eph. 4:1-3, *The Message*)

Are there words or phrases in these verses that speak particularly to you in the way you are presently "walking"? Underline those and spend a few minutes reflecting on them.

Spend two or three minutes reflecting on this statement: Most of us know that we will not be the greatest, but we do not want to be the least.

It is a helpful spiritual discipline to write our prayers, to "pray at the point of a pencil." Do that now. Write a brief prayer, focusing on humility as essential for our Christian walk, and confessing your feelings about *being great* or *not being least.*

DURING THE DAY

How you live today is the primary expression of your life. Seek to invest it in the commitment to "walk worthy of [your] vocation," with humility being a core aspect.

Yesterday you sought for an occasion to be an expression of Christ's life in the world. That is certainly an aspect of walking worthy of your vocation. Continue seeking that possibility today.

How are you coming along with memorizing "And Can It Be That I Should Gain"?

Day 7

CONSTANTLY ABIDING

> I am the real vine; my Father is the vine-dresser. He removes any of my branches which are not bearing fruit and he prunes every branch that does bear fruit to increase its yield. Now, you have already been pruned by my words. You must go on growing in me and I will grow in you. For just as the branch cannot bear any fruit unless it shares the life of the vine, so you can produce nothing unless you go on growing in me. I am the vine itself; you are the branches. It is the [person] who shares my life and whose life I share who proves fruitful. For the plain fact is that apart from me, you can do nothing at all." (John 15:1-5, Phillips*)

One of the things I remember most about my growing-up years in Perry County, Mississippi, is worship in East Side Baptist Church. The services were not well ordered. Brother Grissom, the fifth-grade-educated preacher under whom I was converted, didn't know about such things, but oh, Lord, how he could preach! The services always consisted of singing, praying, and preaching. The quality of music was more than made up for in enthusiasm, congregational participation, and joy. We sang like we meant it. The songs were not preselected. Worshipers had the opportunity to call out their favorite hymn number. And I remember one of my favorites: "Constantly Abiding." I even remember the number in that old hymnal—number 168. The chorus of that song is still alive in my mind, and I often sing it when I'm alone:

> Constantly abiding, Jesus is mine;
> Constantly abiding, rapture divine;
> He never leaves me lonely, whispers, O so kind;
> "I will never leave thee," Jesus is mine.
> (Anne S. Murphy, 1908)

This is what the gospel is all about: life that comes to us now as we allow the presence of Christ to come to full expression in our lives. The vine and the branches are the symbols of our "constantly abiding" metaphor. The life of abiding requires discipline, revolving around the following practices.

Affirm and cultivate awareness of the indwelling Christ. Freedom and joy in our Christian life depend on this. If we believe in the Resurrection, then we must believe that Christ is alive today. He is a current reality. This reality must become personal. Christ is alive in me!

The practice you began on Day 1 of this week, repeating to yourself the secret of Christ in you, is an effective way of affirming and cultivating awareness of the indwelling Christ. I have come to believe that this is the key to Christian experience, certainly the key to authentic Christian piety and spirituality; it is the key to being alive in Christ.

Not only are we to affirm and cultivate awareness of the living Christ; we must also *practice a healthy dependence on Christ.*

My great problem in life is not in not knowing what to do. Most of the time, I'm aware in any given situation of what I ought to do. My problem is to put that knowledge into action. What I need is power. So, it's not enough to affirm and cultivate awareness. We must also *exercise* the indwelling Christ—be dependent upon him and allow him to work in us.

A few years ago, I wrote a sentence describing what I felt was my relationship to Jesus. I said that I was *hopelessly in love with Jesus and helplessly dependent upon him.* To constantly abide in Jesus, we must practice a healthy dependence upon him.

REFLECTING AND RECORDING

One way we constantly abide is to affirm and cultivate an awareness of the indwelling Christ. Think about that in terms of your own life. Has repeating "The secret is simply this . . ." saying to yourself been effective in making you more aware? What about your reading scripture, worshiping, your prayer life? What ongoing disciplines do you need to add to affirm and cultivate awareness of the indwelling Christ? Spend some time with this focused reflection.

A second way we constantly abide is practicing a healthy dependence on Christ. Reflect on whether this is a part of your deliberate spiritual growth.

Is it true that, for the most part, we know what to do; we simply lack the will and the power to do it? What do you think about my confession, *"I am hopelessly in love with Jesus and helplessly dependent upon him"*? After two or three minutes of reflection, write a statement about your feelings in this area of action and dependence.

DURING THE DAY

If you have memorized "And Can It Be That I Should Gain," tell a family member and a close friend what you have been doing as a spiritual discipline. Recite the stanza to them and engage them in a brief conversation about this workbook journey.

Continue observing your day in light of "walking worthy of our vocation." Remember that humility and being an expression of Christ's presence are signs.

GROUP MEETING FOR WEEK THREE

Feedback and follow-up are key ingredients for a Christian fellowship. Feedback keeps the group dynamic working positively for all participants. Follow-up expresses Christian concern and ministry.

The leader is the one primarily responsible for feedback and can elicit it by encouraging all members to share their feelings about how the group is functioning. Listening is crucial. Listening to one another, as much as any other action, affirms others. When we listen to another, we say, "You are important. I value you." Being sure we understand the meaning of what others say is also crucial. We often mishear. Don't hesitate to ask, "Do I hear you saying ____________?" If a couple of persons in a group listen and give feedback in this fashion, they can set the tone for the entire group.

Follow-up is a function for everyone. If we listen to what others say, we will discover needs and concerns beneath the surface, situations that deserve special prayer and attention. Make notes of these as the group shares. Follow up during the week with a telephone call, an encouraging note, or maybe a personal visit. The distinguishing quality of Christian fellowship is caring in action. Ideally, our caring should be so evident that others notice and remark, "My, how those Christians love one another!" Saint Augustine said, "All our good and all our evil certainly lies in the character of our actions. As they are, so are we; for we are the tree, and they the fruit, and, therefore, they prove what each one is" (*A Year with the Saints*, 227). Follow up with each group member.

SHARING TOGETHER

Hopefully, by this time, individuals are beginning to feel safe in the group and perhaps more willing to share. Still, there is no place for pressure. Be sensitive to those who are slow to share. Coax them gently. Every person is a gift to the group.

1. Last week as a "During the Day" exercise, you prayed the hymn "Breathe on Me, Breath of God." Chances are, someone in your group can lead you in singing that

hymn. Turn to the words, if you have not memorized them, and begin your time together with singing.

2. Spend eight to ten minutes allowing each person to talk about "how I'm doing" with this workbook. What is positive? What is negative? Are there special meanings, joys, or difficulties? Don't talk about the content of this week yet; encourage one another.
3. Invite a couple of persons to share an occasion when Jesus' invitation "Come unto me" meant the most to them (Reflecting and Recording, Day 1).
4. Spend a few minutes talking about the connection between Jesus' promise of rest and his invitation, "Take my yoke upon you."
5. Invite a couple of persons to share their experience of either "the rest of pardon," "the rest of acceptance," or "the rest of Jesus' love for me" (Reflecting and Recording, Day 2).
6. Spend five to eight minutes talking about the dual emphasis of Paul: *justification by grace through faith* and the *indwelling Christ*. How have you experienced the church sharing this message?
7. Spend a few minutes talking about the fact that the branches do not suck the sap out of the vine; rather, the vine literally forces its substance into the branches.
8. Invite a couple of people to share what in their lives reflects the presence and power of the indwelling Christ (Reflecting and Recording, Day 4).
9. Have someone read C. S. Lewis's statement from Day 5, and then invite the group to spend a few minutes talking about it. Do group members agree? disagree? What are the implications of Lewis's assertion?

PRAYING TOGETHER

William Law said the following about spiritual disciplines:

"He who has learned to pray has learned the greatest secret of a holy and happy life."

1. Invite the group to share special prayer concerns. After each concern, ask a volunteer to offer a brief prayer.
2. Close your time by praying aloud together this prayer:

Dear Jesus, be present in me in a powerful way as I move though the coming days.
Possess my mind, my heart, my will.
Let no word cross my lips that is not your word.
Let no thoughts be cultivated that are not your thoughts.
Let no deeds be done that are not an expression of your love and concern.
May your presence be real to me in that others will no longer see me but you, Lord Jesus.
May I be cheered by your presence and move through these coming days with no hint of anxiety, so that your peace may flow from my life. Amen.

PRAYER

DAY 1

INSATIABLE HUNGER AND THIRST

O God, you are my God, I seek you,
  my soul thirsts for you;
my flesh faints for you,
  as in a dry and weary land where there is no water.
So I have looked upon you in the sanctuary,
  beholding your power and glory.
Because your steadfast love is better than life,
  my lips will praise you.
So I will bless you as long as I live;
  I will lift up my hands and call on your name.
My soul clings to you;
  your right hand upholds me. (Psalm 63:1-4, 8)

It's time now in our workbook journey to focus specifically on prayer. Our claim is that abiding in Christ is the way of living prayer. We begin with some foundational principles.

First, *desire.*

Desire is power. It is one of the primary forces of life. The deeper the desire, the more powerful it is. Our most consuming desires mold our lives. Great success in life is fueled by intense desire. The people who achieve most are those whose desires are centered and unified.

What is true in all of life is particularly true in our spirituality. Psalm 63 reflects this. "My soul thirsts for you; my flesh faints for you, as in a dry and weary land where there is no water." This is a desperate declaration of the psalmist's dire need for God. It is also a confession of trust and a commitment to praise. The images of thirst and hunger at the beginning of the psalm contrast with the confidence and satisfaction voiced in verse 8: "My soul follows close behind you; your right hand upholds me" (NKJV). A number of translations say, "My soul *clings* to you." One translation paints the picture a bit differently: "My soul followeth hard after thee" (ASV).

The expressions combine not only to portray intense desire but also *will.* When we desire something deeply enough, we *will* it. Emotion and will come together as we invest ourselves completely in achieving it.

One of the characteristics of the saints of the ages, those who have demonstrated an intimate relationship with God, is intense desire; they passionately sought the Lord, followed "hard after" him. When Thomas Aquinas entered the monastery, he desired only to think, to speak, and to hear of God. He dedicated all his works and actions to God. On one occasion he said that God asked him what reward he wanted for the many works he had written. He replied, "No other but Thyself alone, my Lord and my love!"(*A Year with the Saints*, 358).

This echoes the psalmist in Psalm 63, and is expressed vividly in Psalm 42: "As a deer longs for flowing streams, so my soul longs for you, O God. My soul thirsts for God, for the living God" (42:1-2). Here again is a picture of an utterly dried-out person who likens God's presence to life-giving water. It is this dryness, this seemingly unquenchable thirst, that drives us to seek God and fuels our praying.

In a sense, prayer is the deepest impulse of the human soul. Almost as natural as eating and drinking, prayer is an expression of who we basically are. Certainly, as essential as eating and drinking are to our physical well-being, so praying is essential to who we are as whole persons. Sooner or later, sensitive to our insatiable spiritual longing and searching for fulfillment and meaning, we begin to recognize that we cannot depend upon our own resources, or count on our own works, to achieve meaning or to help us grow closer to God.

In his first beatitude, Jesus said that blessed are those who come to that place in their awareness. "Blessed are the poor in spirit, for theirs is the kingdom of heaven" (Matt. 5:3). A. W. Tozer talks about this in terms of "soul poverty," saying, "The way to deeper knowledge of God is through the lonely valleys of *soul poverty* and abnegation of all things. The blessed ones who possess the Kingdom are they who have repudiated every external thing and have rooted from their hearts all sense of possessing. These are the 'poor in spirit.' They have reached an inward state paralleling the outward circumstances of the common beggar in the streets of Jerusalem" (Tozer, *The Pursuit of God*, 23).

For this reason spiritual teachers have often used the parable of the pearl of great price (Matt. 13:45-46) to illustrate our need to passionately seek God. Merchants seeking for riches do not take account of what they have already acquired. Past achievements and possessions are forgotten in their quest for the treasure they now seek. Teachers have also used another comparison for seeking God. They challenge us to act like travelers who do not regard the road they have traveled or the distance they have come but look only to what lies ahead, keeping the destination—our relationship to God—in the center of their vision.

REFLECTING AND RECORDING

The following is a shocking and challenging word from Thomas Merton, a twentieth-century giant in spirituality. He is talking about contemplation as a particular expression of prayer, but his words are relevant to the whole of our prayer life: "It is also true that God often measures His gifts by our desire to receive them, and by our cooperation with His grace, and the Holy

Spirit will not waste any of His gifts on people who have little or no interest in them" (Merton, *What Is Contemplation?*, 8).

Spend some time concentrating on two thoughts of Merton that challenge us. How do you respond? Do you believe this or not? Have you experienced it to any degree in your life? Make some notes in response to each statement.

God's gifts to us are dependent upon our desire to receive them.

The Holy Spirit will not waste any of His gifts on people who have little or no interest in them.

Spend three or four minutes reflecting on Tozer's word: "The way to deeper knowledge of God is through the lonely valleys of soul poverty and abnegation of all things." Make some notes about how you have experienced or are experiencing *soul poverty*.

One of my favorite writers, Brennan Manning, a former Catholic priest, recovering alcoholic, and one who is painfully honest about his soul poverty, shares a challenging blessing, written by his former spiritual director, Larry Hein. Read this prayer slowly and receive it as a personal blessing.

> May all your expectations be frustrated, may all your plans be thwarted, may all your desires be withered into nothingness, that you may experience the powerlessness and poverty of a child and sing and dance in the love of God who is Father, Son, and Spirit. And today on planet Earth, may you experience the wonder and beauty of yourself as Abba's child and temple of the Holy Spirit through Jesus Christ our Lord (Manning with Jim Hancock, *Posers, Fakers, and Wannabes*, 10).

DURING THE DAY

The New Living Translation of Psalm 27:7-8 is printed on page 203. Cut it out and carry it with you for the next few days. Use every opportunity each day to read it in order to memorize it. Let it be your prayer. We will consider this psalm on Day 3 of this week.

Day 2

DRAWN BY THE FATHER

> Then the Jews began to complain about him because he said, "I am the bread that came down from heaven." They were saying, "Is not this Jesus, the son of Joseph, whose father and mother we know? How can he now say, 'I have come down from heaven'?" Jesus answered them, "Do not complain among yourselves. No one can come to me unless drawn by the Father who sent me." (John 6:41-44)

Yesterday we considered our insatiable hunger and thirst for God as the basic energy that fuels our praying. Prayer is the deepest impulse of the human soul. Almost as natural as eating and drinking, prayer is an expression of who we basically are. Certainly, as essential as eating and drinking are to our physical well-being, praying is essential to who we are as whole persons.

Our longing for God is a gift from God. Though we may not have thought of it in this fashion, our hunger and thirst for God are an expression of God's grace. Jesus said to those who were complaining about his teaching, "No one can come to me unless drawn by the Father who sent me." He had said to them, "I am the bread of life. Whoever comes to me will never be hungry, and whoever believes in me will never be thirsty" (John 6:35). Just like their forebears in the wilderness who were unable to accept the manna as a gracious gift from God, sustaining them "for the day," and not needing to store up or hoard it, Jesus' listeners couldn't understand. Jesus used this occasion of misunderstanding and unbelief to make the case for grace and our need to be "drawn by the Father."

Being "drawn by the Father" does not affirm arbitrary action on God's part, or anything that would suggest predestination. It underscores the need for divine grace to generate faith within us. John Wesley referred to the "strong and sweet, yet still resistible, motions of [God's] heavenly grace" (*John Wesley's Notes on the Bible*, 6:44). In theological language we call it *prevenient grace.* Wesley talked about grace impinging upon us and working in three specific ways: prevenient grace, justifying grace, and sanctifying grace. Prevenient grace is the grace of God that goes before us, pulling us, wooing us, seeking to open our minds and hearts, and eventually giving us faith. Justifying grace is the forgiving love of God, freely given to us, reconciling us, putting us right with God, making Christ, who knew no sin, to be sin on our behalf. Sanctifying grace is the work and spirit of Christ within us, restoring the broken image of God, completing the salvation that was begun in justification, and bringing us to complete newness of life, and perfection in love.

As we considered on Days 1 and 2 of Week 1, God's movement toward us is all grace. Prevenient grace means that before we can seek God, God must first have sought us. We seek the Lord because the Lord has sought us. Before we have any conscious experience of divine grace, grace is present, working in our lives even before we are aware of it. As clear as anything else in the Bible is the fact that God not only seeks us but, in fact, relentlessly pursues us. Our hunger and thirst for God actually originates with God. No one is excluded from the work of prevenient grace. Grace is a gift of God *for all.* Our deliberate seeking, the practice of spiritual disciplines—including prayer—is the outworking of the longing God has put within us. Prayer is both gift and discipline.

Yesterday we noted how the psalmist referred to God as the life-giving water that quenches our thirst. John records Jesus' claim that he is the water that satisfies our eternal longing. The woman at the well in Samaria had come to draw water. She was aware that the water she desperately needed to satisfy her raging thirst was not in that well. She resonated with Jesus' response to her: "Those who drink of the water that I will give them will never be thirsty. The water that I will give will become in them a spring of water gushing up to eternal life" (John 4:14).

When you put this claim of Jesus beside his claim with which we began—"No one can come to me unless drawn by the Father who sent me"—you have dynamics that are essential for abiding in Christ as the way of living prayer. Prayer is not our own doing alone; God draws us to himself—and he draws us through Christ. Christ is the living water that alone will satisfy our spiritual thirst. Abiding in Christ, then, is not only the dynamic of living prayer; it is also the dynamic of our Christian walk. Everything depends on our right relationship to Christ. A casual sweep through Paul's letters in the New Testament confirms this. "In all these things we are more than conquerors through him who loved us" (Rom. 8:37). "Thanks be to God, who in Christ always leads us in triumphal procession, and through us spreads in every place the fragrance that comes from knowing him" (2 Cor. 2:14).

In Christ we find all we need for a life of abundant grace. But remember, prayer is both a gift and a discipline. Though prayer is a privilege and not a duty, discipline is required for cultivating a prayerful life.

Most of us, when we practice prayer as a duty, allow the discipline to take the joy and spontaneity out of prayer. It is crucial to see discipline not just as "a religious requirement" but as the way to spiritual growth and ultimately our total transformation.

The words *discipline* and *disciple* are connected. A disciple is someone who subscribes to the teachings of a master and helps spread those teachings. Any adherent of a movement may be called a disciple. *Discipline* is variously defined as training intended to produce a specified character or pattern of behavior. From another perspective, *discipline* may be seen as punishment intended to correct or train, or it may be a set of rules or methods.

In the context of the Christian faith, a disciple is not only one who subscribes to the teachings of Jesus and seeks to spread them, but also one who seeks to relive Jesus' life in the world. Discipline for the Christian is the way we train ourselves or allow the Spirit to train us to be "like Jesus," to appropriate his spirit, and to cultivate the power to live his life in the world (Dunnam, *The Workbook on Spiritual Disciplines*, 15).

Recall now our definition of prayer. *Prayer is recognizing, cultivating awareness of, and giving expression to the indwelling Christ.* By recognizing I mean more than affirming Christ's presence. That is the beginning, of course. But *living* prayer is more. Through meditation, reflection, living with scripture, corporate worship, intentional relationship and conversation with others, and other spiritual disciplines, we cultivate our awareness of Christ's presence within us. We sharpen our sensitivity and deepen our yieldedness to his presence. We can then give expression to the indwelling Christ, actually reflecting his presence within us in our daily living.

REFLECTING AND RECORDING

Prevenient grace is the grace of God going before us. Before we can seek God, God must have first sought us. Recall an experience of God's prevenient grace in your life—your knowing in retrospect that God was seeking you, leading you, going before you before you were aware of, or had acknowledged God's grace. Make enough notes here to get that experience clearly in mind.

Spend some time responding to these questions: Do I view prayer as duty and obligation? Do I work hard at prayer? How can I cultivate the gift of abundant grace and begin to practice prayer as a gift?

Spend a few minutes reflecting on this claim: Abiding in Christ . . . is not only the *dynamic of living prayer; it is also the dynamic of the Christian walk.*

Write a few sentences about how you have seen and experienced prayer either as a duty or a gift, or both.

DURING THE DAY

Continue praying Psalm 27:7-8 (found on page 203).

Day 3

"LORD, I AM COMING"

The Lord is my light and my salvation; whom shall I fear?
The Lord is the stronghold of my life; of whom shall I be afraid?

. . . .

Though an army encamp against me, my heart shall not fear;
though war rise up against me, yet I will be confident.

One thing I asked of the Lord, that will I seek after:
to live in the house of the Lord all the days of my life,
to behold the beauty of the Lord, and to inquire in his temple.

For he will hide me in his shelter in the day of trouble;
he will conceal me under the cover of his tent;
he will set me high on a rock.

. . . .

Hear, O Lord, when I cry aloud, be gracious to me and answer me!
"Come," my heart says, "seek his face!"
Your face, Lord, do I seek. (Psalm 27:1, 3-5, 7-8)

Psalm 27 is one of my favorite psalms, and it's the favorite of many. I don't know when, but it was a long time ago when I memorized verse 1 from the King James Version: "The Lord is my light and my salvation: whom shall I fear? The Lord is the strength of my life; of whom shall I be afraid?"

Two words in the psalm resonate in all of our lives: fear and confidence. Both words are in this almost unbelievable testimony of verse 3. That's the reason it is a favorite verse for so many.

I recently claimed another passage in this psalm as a favorite. It probably would not have happened had I not been reading a new translation. My wife, Jerry, and I were using the *New Living Translation* in our daily devotional time together. And there it was, verses 7 and 8. In this study, you have been praying these verses for the past two days:

> Hear me as I pray, O LORD.
> Be merciful and answer me!
> My heart has heard you say, "Come and talk with me."
> And my heart responds, "LORD, I am coming." (Ps. 27:7-8, NLT)

What a beautiful expression of the very foundation of prayer. Prayer is not foreign to our human nature. It is perhaps the deepest impulse of the human soul. We pray because it's part of who we are. It is related to our search for meaning, our longing for relationship and intimacy, and our need to grow. However it is practiced, prayer is an expression of our hunger for God. Inclination to prayer is a part of our native endowment, so it is natural and universal.

In all our thinking about prayer, it is good to stay aware of the fact that prayer is God's idea. The psalmist had heard correctly: "My heart has heard you say, 'Come and talk with me.'" What a beautiful response, so simple and sincere: "Lord, I am coming." Prayer is God's idea.

At first glance, that statement may not sound so important. But think about it. Prayer raises some tough questions.

What about the sovereignty of God? Isn't God going to do whatever God wants, whether we pray or not?

What about the free will of persons? Much of our praying is directed toward the needs, decisions, and directions of others. How do we expect our praying to impact their freedom? Why should we pray for persons to become Christian who don't want to be Christian?

What about healing? Does our praying make any difference? What kind of difference? And why are some people for whom we pray healed while others are not?

These are tough questions. Questions like these prevent many people from praying. That's the reason we consider the notion that prayer is God's idea. In a sense, that is the reason I pray. Think about it, and don't consider me irreverent for suggesting it: All the questions, objections, and contradictions surrounding prayer—and they are many and monumental—all of them are God's problems, not mine; because prayer is God's idea. God has commanded us to pray.

I'm not suggesting that we don't have to wrestle with the questions, problems, and contradictions surrounding prayer. I'm simply saying that we don't have to solve the problems or answer the questions in order to pray. They are God's problems, and God has commanded us to pray.

Over and over again in scripture, God calls us to pray. The memorable expression of it in the Old Testament is 2 Chronicles 7:14: "If my people who are called by my name humble themselves, pray, seek my face, and turn from their wicked ways, then I will hear from heaven, and will forgive their sin and heal their land."

The New Testament issues the call to pray in different ways. There is the parable of the widow and the unjust judge. The widow kept coming to the judge, begging him to grant her justice against her opponent. Again and again, she came, but the judge kept refusing to pay attention to her plea. The poor widow refused to give up, and the judge finally responded with this explanation: "Though I have no fear of God and no respect for anyone, yet because this widow keeps bothering me, I will grant her justice, so that she may not wear me out by continually coming" (Luke 18:4-5).

The parable invites a lot of thought and commentary. Certainly, Jesus was not teaching that God is like that judge. He was teaching about persistence in prayer. Luke introduces the parable with this sentence: "Then Jesus told them a parable about their need to pray always and not to lose heart" (18:1).

So, prayer is God's idea. No matter what the problems, questions, objections, or contradictions, God calls us to pray. What a beautiful response of the psalmist. "My heart has heard you say, 'Come and talk with me.' And my heart responds, 'Lord, I am coming'" (Ps. 27:8, NLT).

Reflect on three simple affirmations that are profoundly relevant to prayer:

1. *God cares what happens to us.* I believe this with all my heart. I know that not all signs indicate that. Sometimes our lives fall to pieces, and we are not sure that there is a God, much less a God who cares for us. We must remember that God is not responsible for what happens to us. There is sin and evil and human freedom—all of which are intimately linked—that bring much of the chaos, confusion, and contradictions, as well as pain and suffering, into our lives. Though life is unfair, God is good. God cares what happens to us.

2. *God hears us when we pray.* Is anything more important than to be listened to? As we celebrated in Weeks 1 and 2, our clearest picture of God is Jesus. One of the most pronounced characteristics of Jesus' life and ministry was the attention he gave to people around him. He heard blind Bartimaeus call out from the roadside. He felt the touch of the woman who had been hemorrhaging for twelve years when she reached out in the crowd and managed to touch just the hem of his robe. He saw Zacchaeus up in the sycamore tree. He listened to the leper who came to him and said, "If you choose, you can make me clean." One of the most tender words in scripture is Jesus' response to that leper. In the Phillips translation he says, "Of course I want to—be clean!"* Since God is like Jesus, we know that God hears us when we pray.

---

3. *God answers us.* Just as surely as we speak to God, as we seek God, as we seek to be related to God—God responds to us. The prophet Isaiah recorded a marvelous word of the Lord that speaks to this issue. "Before they call I will answer, while they are yet speaking I will hear" (Isa. 65:24). What an extravagant word—God hears and answers. Even before the woman who had the issue of blood said anything, as she reached out in faith and touched the hem of Jesus' robe, he responded. What a bracing word as we consider our praying: *God answers.*

REFLECTING AND RECORDING

Spend a few minutes reflecting on why the claim that prayer is God's idea is important.

Write two or three sentences of affirmation/doubt/response/questions in response to the following statements.

God cares what happens to us.

God hears us when we pray.

God answers us.

DURING THE DAY

Continue praying the "Lord, I am coming" prayer (page 203). Have you have memorized it?

Practice some deliberate Christian conferencing this week by finding someone who is not a part of your workbook group (if you are in a group) and ask for his or her response to the notion that *prayer is God's idea.* Be prepared to share the fact that prayer raises serious questions about the nature of God, about healing, and human freedom.

Day 4

FUNDAMENTALS: ADORATION, PRAISE, AND THANKSGIVING

I will bless the LORD at all times;
his praise shall continually be in my mouth.
My soul makes its boast in the LORD;
let the humble hear and be glad.
O magnify the LORD with me,
and let us exalt his name together. (Psalm 34:1-3)

Yesterday I made the point that prayer is both a gift and discipline. It is one of the primary spiritual disciplines in growing us up into Christlikeness.

While this workbook journey is specifically focused on abiding in Christ as the way of living prayer, we focus for a few days on some fundamentals of prayer, rehearsing a bit the content of *The Workbook of Living Prayer*. It is not difficult to identify in scripture elements that are essential to prayer. One of the memorable ways these elements have been identified is in the acronym ACTS: adoration, confession, thanksgiving and supplication.

It doesn't matter where we begin, continue, or end in our praying, these elements are essential. Let's consider them.

Adoration and praise are one dynamic. One way of thinking about it is *we adore God for who God is; we praise God for what God has done and is doing*. "O magnify the LORD with me, and let us exalt his name together," David shouted in Psalm 34. The Psalms are full of such exultations of adoration and praise.

This movement of prayer is essential because it moves us out of ourselves and our own situation into the realm of God's grace and power. We bring our whole self—all that we are—to praise God. "Bless the LORD, O my soul, and all that is within me, bless his holy name"(Ps. 103:1). In Hebrew the word for *bless* is *barachi*, and it originally meant "to bend the knee before," that is, to bow and offer homage to one's king, one's sovereign. When we express our adoration and praise, we are bowing before our God, knowing that all life, *our* life, belongs to God. We praise God for redemption, healing, reconciliation, and forgiveness, because that is what God has done. We adore God for God's mercy, justice, lovingkindness, providential care—for that is who God is.

Psalm 34:2 states a truth we acknowledge when adoration and praise punctuate our praying. "My soul makes its boast in the LORD; let the humble hear and be glad." The ground for any "boasting" is not in ourselves, either our accomplishments or reputation, but in the greatness of God. "O magnify the LORD with me," David sang. *Magnify* does not mean to make God big but to recognize and acknowledge who God is. The NIV translates that verse as "Glorify the LORD with me." When we see God as God is, we *glorify* him.

In our praying this means that *we do not tell God how big our mountains are; we tell our mountains how big God is.* There is power in this kind of praise-praying. Return to that Hebrew word, *barachi*, which means "to bless or adore." The root word *barak* means "to kneel, bless, kneel down." It is the word Job used in Job 1:21: "Blessed be (*barak*) the name of the Lord." Recall the occasion. Job had been reduced to nothing, his servants murdered, his flocks killed, his children lost in a great tornado. He was physically and emotionally devastated, but not spiritually. He "arose, tore his robe, shaved his head and fell on the ground and worshiped"(1:20). Then he said, "Naked I came from my mother's womb, and naked shall I return there; the LORD gave, and the LORD has taken away; blessed be the name of the LORD"(1:21).

To praise God in the midst of tragedy, suffering, defeat, and loss is to find the source of power to overcome, and if not to overcome, then to be sustained in the midst of every circumstance. Adoration and praise take our eyes off our own problems and limitations and enable us to see and receive the limitless resources of the Holy Spirit.

Confession is the second essential in the ACTS of prayer. We will focus there tomorrow; for now, a brief word about *thanksgiving*.

There is little difference between praise and thanksgiving. We said earlier that we adore God for who God is; we praise God for what God is doing. Thanksgiving is the particular expression of praise—thanking God for the specific things he is doing.

An attitude of gratitude needs to permeate our praying. We can cultivate this attitude by reliving our day and identifying situations and people in our lives for which we are grateful. To be sure, there may be some days when everything seems a curse rather than a blessing. We must not be daunted by these days, for if we are disciplined in prayer, we will have cultivated our perception, and we will have stored up memories of all that for which we can be joyfully thankful.

REFLECTING AND RECORDING

As an act of adoration and praise, write one or two sentences after each of the psalm verses, putting the psalm in your own words, or expressing a feeling the psalm inspires.

"O magnify the LORD with me, and let us exalt his name together" (Ps. 34:3).

"Bless the Lord, O my soul, and all that is within me; bless his holy name" (Ps. 103:1).

"Your steadfast love, O Lord, extends to the heavens, your faithfulness to the clouds" (Ps. 36:5).

"It is good to give thanks to the Lord, to sing praises to your name, O Most High; to declare your steadfast love in the morning, and your faithfulness by night" (Ps. 92:1-2).

List some good things that have happened to you in the past two weeks.

Have you thanked God for these good things? If not, do so now.

Recall your most recent experience of tragedy, loss, suffering, or defeat. Make some notes to get that experience clearly in mind.

What was your praying like during that time? Were praise and adoration part of it? Would more praise and adoration made a positive difference? Now, in the aftermath and memory of that experience, spend some time praising God. If you find this difficult, it's okay. Praise God as you can.

DURING THE DAY

Did you conference yesterday with someone about the assertion that prayer is God's idea? If not, do so today.

Spiritual guides have taught us to use what they call *prayers of aspiration*. These are simply brief, spontaneous exclamations to the Lord, sometimes called "arrow" prayers. Spend enough time right now to get Psalm 103:1 (printed under Reflecting and Recording) in your mind. It will confirm God's presence and add a special flavor to your life if you will repeat it often throughout the day. Simply register it in your mind or repeat it in silence, but I find it meaningful when the situation allows, to blurt it out loud. You might want to think of particular occasions when it will be natural to offer the prayer.

DAY 5

FUNDAMENTALS: CONFESSION AND SUPPLICATION

Have mercy on me, O God,
  according to your steadfast love;
according to your abundant mercy
  blot out my transgressions.
Wash me thoroughly from my iniquity,
  and cleanse me from my sin.

For I know my transgressions,
  and my sin is ever before me.
Against you, you alone, have I sinned,

and done what is evil in your sight,
so that you are justified in your sentence
and blameless when you pass judgment.
Indeed, I was born guilty,
a sinner when my mother conceived me. (Psalm 51:1-5)

Self-examination and confession go together as a discipline for cultivating Christlikeness. This dynamic is an essential element of prayer.

We are masters of self-deceit and deceitfulness. This seems to be a part of the human condition. In many ways, others see us much more clearly than we see ourselves. Self-examination and confession keep us aware of our true condition.

One of the greatest barriers to spiritual well-being and emotional wholeness is being unaware of, or unconscious of, or even unwilling to recognize and admit our sin and guilt. First John 1:8 says, "If we claim to be sinless, we are self-deceived and strangers to the truth." That's the New English Bible translation. The New Revised Standard Version makes it even stronger: "If we say that we have no sin, we deceive ourselves, and *the truth is not in us*" (italics added). This is a tough word. John goes on to say, "If we say that we have not sinned, we make [God] a liar" (1 John 1:10).

Confession is essential because our greatest need is forgiveness. Forgiveness requires repentance, and repentance requires confession. The verses we began with are the beginning of the Bible's most vivid case. The psalm has been credited to King David. Giving in to his lust, he took for himself Bathsheba, the beautiful wife of Uriah, and then had Uriah killed. What had begun as lust resulted in adultery and murder, which were too much for David to deal with.

The misery, spiritual pain, and agony were maddening until the prophet Nathan confronted the king with his sin, and David knew God was the one to whom he had to answer. His need to confess was necessary if he was to experience what he needed most: *forgiveness.*

David uses three words to picture the different aspects of sin. *Pesha* means "rebellion," "transgression"—setting oneself against the will and law of God. It is an act of high treason against the sovereign of the universe. *Avon*, "iniquity," means that which is "twisted" or "warped" or "crooked." It is depravity of conduct. The third word, *chatah*, "sin," means literally "missing the aim or the mark."

David recognized that sin is something that happened on the inside before it expressed itself outwardly. As a part of his confession and repentance, he prayed, "You desire truth in the inward being; therefore teach me wisdom in my secret heart" (51:6). God must do something for David that he can't do for himself. David uses verbs like "blot out" and "wash me thoroughly" as he anguishes for God to do whatever it will take to make him acceptable in God's sight.

Confession means living truthfully. John Wesley contended that to live truthfully is a mark of God's grace in our lives. The witness of scripture is that the dominant desire of God's heart is forgiveness. Confession is essential because our sins separate us from God. Isaiah said, "But your iniquities have made a separation between you and your God, And your sins have hidden his face from you so that He does not hear (Isa. 59:2, NASB). But sin does not have to separate us from God. John said, "If we confess our sins, he is faithful and just and will forgive us our sins and purify us from all unrighteousness" (1 John 1:9, NIV). The truth is, confession is a prerequisite, not to God's forgiveness, but to our receiving God's forgiveness.

Adoration, confession, and thanksgiving prepare us for *supplication*. This is an intense word and combines what we may refer to as petition and intercession in our praying. Paul included supplication as an essential of prayer in his instruction for our daily living: "Do not worry about anything, but in everything by prayer and *supplication* with thanksgiving let your requests be made known to God" (Phil. 4:6, emphasis added). We are going to give more attention to this idea in Week 6 when we focus on "an intercessory life." For now, think of it in terms of turning our whole being toward God.

> Sometimes we come [to God] with calm and confidence, yet how often do we come with doubts and questions. We bring praise, but also we come in pain. Whether we acknowledge, anger and fear may be in our minds and hearts as much as reverence and awe. We may come to sit still in God's presence, or we may have to wrestle with the angel as Jacob did and refuse to let go until we get a blessing. Supplication is a part of our praying. We are limited for words to express our thanksgiving; but there are times when our feelings are so raw, our concerns so overwhelming, our passion so intense, we can do little more than anguish in the presence of God. We're waiting for the biopsy report of a loved one, or an inexplicable accident drives us to doubt a loving God. A broken friendship leaves us lonely and emotionally distraught. (Maxie Dunnam and John David Walt Jr., *Praying the Story*, 31).

So, in prayer we turn our whole being toward God.

REFLECTING AND RECORDING

Spend a few minutes reflecting on sin in terms of the different aspects David gave it in his confession.

Rebellion or transgression—setting ourselves against God's law and/or law

Iniquity—that which is twisted, warped, or crooked, depravity of conduct

Sin—missing the mark

Spend a couple of minutes pondering this thought: Confession is a prerequisite, not to God's forgiveness, but to our receiving God's forgiveness.

Self-examination and confession go together. Look at yourself in light of the above aspects of sin, and write a prayer of confession focused on how you see yourself before God right now.

Reread the paragraph concerning *supplication*.

Spend the balance of your time in supplication.

DURING THE DAY

Continue the practice of "arrow" prayers, using the prayer "Bless the Lord, O my soul." Add to it: "Lord Jesus Christ, Son of God, have mercy on me a sinner." Take enough time now to get it firmly in your mind. Praying both together is an act of adoration/praise and confession.

Day 6

NAMING AND BEING NAMED

Lord, you have been our dwelling-place
  in all generations.
Before the mountains were brought forth,
  or ever you had formed the earth and the world,
  from everlasting to everlasting you are God. (Psalm 90:1-2)

It was 1993. My friend Leonard Sweet, then president of United Theological Seminary, organized a group of pastors for a visit to Russia. History-shaping events were taking place. Because of his *perestroika* ideology, Mikhail Gorbachev had been ousted as president of the Soviet Union and replaced by Boris Yeltsin.

There were eighteen of us, all from the United States except Bishop Sundo Kim, pastor of the then-largest Methodist church in the world in Seoul, Korea. We were given an audience with former president Gorbachev. Protocol was well defined. Though we were known as Christians, this was to be an "educational," not a "religious" conversation. We were given one hour, which meant planning our time well. We devised a series of questions and designated the persons who were to ask the questions. Since we wanted to honor the "religious restriction," yet wanted to at least make a Christian statement of support and concern, Bishop Kim was assigned the task of simply making a closing statement, scripted to go something like this: "Mr. President, thank you for sharing with us. We are grateful for your leadership, and especially the last few years, fostering *perestroika*. We are Christian ministers, and we want you to know our prayers are with you as you take another path of leadership in your country."

It was a memorable meeting, with lively conversation and surprising openness on the part of Mr. Gorbachev. The meeting lasted for over two hours, rather than the one hour we had been promised.

We were seated around a conference table—the president at the head of the table, his assistant to his left, my friend Bishop Kim to his immediate right, and I was seated next to Bishop Kim. It became obvious that Gorbachev was "winding down," and his assistant was anxious to close the meeting, so the signal was given to Bishop Kim to make our closing statement.

Bishop Kim is not a "script" person and is very sensitive to the Holy Spirit. He surprised us all by breaking the "rules" we had established, saying something like this: "Mr. President, we understand that your mother is a Christian, that you were baptized as a baby, and that your mother prays for you daily. Is this true?"

Gorbachev's shock was registered in the blush on his face, but he recovered in a moment and, much to our surprise, began to talk rather freely. "Yes, that's true," he said. "My mother is a Christian." He tried to make light of the issue and move away from what he thought might become a serious discussion. He told us that at birth he had been named Victor. With a sly smile, he wondered aloud how things might have been different had he retained that name, given what had so recently happened to him—having been ousted from the presidency. He smiled broadly and concluded, "At my baptism, I was given the Christian name Mikhail (Michael)." He paused very deliberately, smiled broadly again, and concluded: "As you must know, Mikhail is not a bad name. You know, it means 'messenger of God.' Who knows which might be better? Victor or Mikhail?"

Bishop Kim couldn't let that go. "Thank you so much, Mr. President. We are proud of your mother, and we know her prayers have made a difference and will continue to make a difference in your life. And we are going to pray for you. I'm going to ask Dr. Dunnam to pray for you right now."

I've never been asked to pray in such a surprising way. John Wesley's advice to his Methodist preachers became a reality: "Always be ready," he said," to pray, preach, or die." I prayed.

I remembered all this when I read a news item fifteen years later (March 19, 2008). The headline got my attention: FORMER SOVIET LEADER PROFESSES FAITH IN GOD. The story recorded the fact that Mikhail Gorbachev "publicly acknowledged his Christian faith for the first time on March 19 during a visit to the tomb of Saint Francis of Assisi."

The story makes the case that prayer does make a difference (I'm thinking primarily of Gorbachev's mother's prayers), though there have been contradictory witnesses. I tell the story to make the case for a way of praying: *naming and being named.* It was clear that Mr. Gorbachev's name was important to him. Naming is important. It designates our identity, and nothing is more important than knowing who we are.

God's activity throughout history has involved naming. Beginning with Adam and Eve, God has called people by name; God addressed Abraham, Moses, the prophets—naming them; God called Cain, by name, to accountability, "Where is your brother Abel?" The *covenant* was a naming event. Hosea captured God's words: "I will have mercy upon her who had not obtained mercy; Then I will say to those who were not My people, 'You are my people!'" (2:23, NKJV). So Israel is called into being, a nation named as God's people.

The coming of Jesus is the ultimate in God's naming activity. It wasn't enough for God to name himself as the God of Abraham, Isaac, and Jacob. He had to become an Abraham, Isaac, or Jacob. He did, and his name is Jesus.

This is the activity of God in history—*naming*. This is also what prayer is all about: *naming and being named.* We will continue thinking about this dynamic tomorrow.

REFLECTING AND RECORDING

Take a few minutes to scan our discussion of the incarnation on Day 3 of Week 1. After doing so, bask—sun yourself—in this most unique core truth of the Christian faith: *It wasn't enough for God to name himself as the God of Abraham, Isaac, and Jacob. He had to become an Abraham, Isaac, or Jacob. He did, and his name is Jesus.*

One memorable Old Testament story is in 1 Kings 19. The prophet Elijah was "worn out" from much labor, despondent and depressed because his work as God's messenger was seemingly futile. He was also fearful of Jezebel. He fled all the way from northern Israel to Beer-sheba, one of the southernmost cities of Judah. Elijah then sought seclusion and safety in a cave on Mount Horeb. Not only was he seeking to escape from the forces of Jezebel, but he was, in effect, trying to discover God's will or leave behind his work as God's prophet.

> There on Mount Horeb came a mighty wind, so strong that it was breaking rocks in pieces and splitting the mountain, but the Lord was not in the wind. Then came the earthquake, but the Lord was not in the tumultuous quake. After the earthquake came the fire, but the Lord was not in the heat or the blaze. After these cataclysmic upheavals, there was the "sound of sheer silence." Then the prophet heard, "What are you doing here, Elijah?"

Try to find time today to read the whole story from 1 Kings 19. The first direct revelation of God involves calling Elijah by his personal name. That was redemption and renewal for Elijah.

Spend a few minutes pondering the importance of naming and being named. Think of it in terms of what we know about God's activity in history—calling people by name. Think of it in terms of your being known by name.

Recall one of your most important experiences of being known and called by name. Make enough notes to get the details, but more important, the feeling of that experience fresh in mind.

DURING THE DAY

Continue practicing "arrow" prayers.

DAY 7

NOT A SERVANT BUT A SON

> This is my commandment, that you love one another as I have loved you. No one has greater love than this, to lay down one's life for one's friends. You are my friends if you do what I

command you. I do not call you servants any longer, because the servant does not know what the master is doing; but I have called you friends, because I have made known to you everything that I have heard from my Father. You did not choose me but I chose you. And I appointed you to go and bear fruit, fruit that will last, so that the Father will give you whatever you ask him in my name. I am giving you these commands so that you may love one another. (John 15:12-17)

We closed our reflection yesterday by suggesting that a primary dynamic of prayer is *naming and being named.* I mentioned that *naming* is one of God's activities in history. That naming goes on, even beyond the Incarnation, reaching a beautiful climax in the theme text of this workbook journey, John 15. Jesus tells us who God is and who he is in relation to God. "I am the true vine, and my Father is the vine-grower" (v. 1). Then he tells us who he is and who we are in relation to him. "I am the vine, you are the branches" (v. 5).

After his beautiful and challenging teaching about our relationship to him and to the Father, Jesus speaks very concretely about his expectation of those who would be his followers. He takes the dynamic to its limit when he says to his followers: "I do not call you servants any longer . . . but I have called you friends" (v. 15).

We are named, not as slaves or servants but as children of God. Think about what this means for our praying. God, who is "high and lifted up," has come to us in Jesus Christ. Through Jesus' life, death, and resurrection, the veil of the temple—the veil that closed off the holy of holies into which only the high priest could go—has been torn from top to bottom. The holy of holies, the very heart of God, is now open to all.

Prayer is relationship. It is meeting. It is being with God. It is naming and being named. I've heard this relationship described as one in which we move from a hello of politeness to an embrace of love (Ann Rauvola Bailey, *Personal Prayers*, 5). Consider these dynamics of naming and being named as a way of praying.

First, *we name God for ourselves*, as God is in our experience. This includes, of course, adoration and praise, but also the honest expression of how we are experiencing God in the present. In a sense, this may reflect more of who we are than who God is.

The Psalms provide a good, sometimes even shocking, demonstration of this dynamic.

But you, O Lord, are a shield around me,
my glory, and the one who lifts up my head. (3:3)

O Lord, do not rebuke me in your anger,
or discipline me in your wrath. (6:1)

The Lord is my shepherd, I shall not want. (23:1)

In you, O Lord, I seek refuge;
do not let me ever be put to shame;
in your righteousness deliver me. (31:1)

The psalmist doesn't pretend. He names God out of experience, calling out from the depth of himself. At one time he may be exulting, O God, "in your presence there is fullness of joy" (Ps. 16:11), or "I love you, O LORD, my strength" (Ps. 18:1). At another time he may be anguishing, "O my God, I cry by day, but you do not answer" (22:2), or O God, "do not let me be put to shame" (Ps. 31:17).

As you can see, this naming of God reflects *supplication*, as well as praise and thanksgiving. Psalm 69 is a dramatic example of supplication, turning one's whole being toward God. The psalmist confesses that he is in "deep water, and the floods overwhelm" him (v. 2, NLT). Then he says, "I am exhausted from crying for help; my throat is parched. My eyes are swollen with weeping, waiting for my God to help me" (v. 3, NLT). Yet, after all that, he ends up in trust and confidence. "I will praise the name of God with a song; I will magnify him with thanksgiving. . . . For the LORD hears the need and does not despise his own that are in bonds"(vv. 30, 33).

The second dynamic of naming is *naming ourselves before God*. This is confession and repentance, as we discussed on Day 5, but it is more. It is honestly locating ourselves as we are before God. That means the good and the bad, the pain and the joy, the struggle and the achievement, the defeat and the victory. Here is one of the clearest examples of it I know.

One night during the tension of the Montgomery bus boycott, just as Dr. Martin Luther King Jr. was about to doze off, the phone rang. He picked it up and heard an angry voice say, "Listen, nigger, we've taken all we want from you. Before next week you'll be sorry you ever came to Montgomery." King hung up, but he couldn't sleep. Fear gripped him. He described what happened next:

> I got out of bed and began to walk the floor. Finally, I went to the kitchen and heated a pot of coffee. I was ready to give up. I tried to think of a way to move out of the picture without appearing to be a coward. In this state of exhaustion, when my courage had almost gone, I determined to take my problem to God. My head in my hands, I bowed over the kitchen table and prayed aloud. The words I spoke to God that midnight are still vivid in my memory. "I am here taking a stand for what I believe is right. But now I am afraid. The people are looking to me for leadership, and if I stand before them without strength and courage, they too will falter. I am at the end of my powers. I have nothing left. I've come to the point where I can't face it alone." (Martin Luther King Jr., *Strength to Love*, 196–97)

King talked honestly to God, as Jesus did on the cross when he prayed: "My God, my God, why have you forsaken me?" (Matt. 27:46) and "Father, into your hands I commend my spirit" (Luke 23:46). Just as any relationship requires honest sharing to be authentic, so this kind of naming is essential in our relationship with God—in our praying.

The third dynamic of naming essential in our prayer relationship is *allowing God to name us*.

This is probably the most neglected dimension of our praying—being silent, alone with God, opening ourselves to be named by God. A dramatic biblical example of this dynamic is Jacob. All night long he wrestled with the Lord's emissary. How long do we wait in silence in our praying? Do we wrestle? We speak and then we move on as though we had prayed. But Jacob did not give up so easily. His was an all-night struggle, and do you remember what happened? He got a new name. No longer would he be called Jacob, meaning "supplanter or deceiver," but Israel, or "God wrestler."

In prayer, we wait in the presence of the Lord, to be named, to receive God's blessing or judgment, comfort or challenge. It is only when we locate ourselves honestly before God and wait receptively that God speaks, and we hear and receive what he wishes to offer.

Let's return to the story of Dr. Martin Luther King Jr. After he had named himself before God, God named him. Here is the balance of his testimony.

> At that moment I experienced the presence of the Divine as I had never before experienced him. It seemed as though I could hear the quiet assurance of an inner voice, saying, "Stand up for righteousness, stand up for truth. God will be at your side forever." Almost at once my fears began to pass from me. My uncertainty disappeared. I was ready to face anything. (Ibid., 197)

REFLECTING AND RECORDING

Read again the Psalm passages above where the psalmist is naming God for himself.

In a sentence or two, name God as you are presently experiencing God.

Now honestly locate yourself before God. It may not be a confession of sin or a cry of need. It may be an expression of joy, a shout of praise, or an exclamation of surprise at the grace of God becoming real to you.

Sit quietly now for four or five minutes. Seek to hear God speaking to you. Remember that God speaks through your *mind*, giving you an idea, or a thought; God speaks through your *emotion*, stirring up feelings; God speaks through *memory*, reminding you of a previous experience, a previous "naming" of you. Record what you experience.

DURING THE DAY

As you move through the day, seek to be sensitive to God's speaking—through your mind, emotions, or memory.

GROUP MEETING FOR WEEK FOUR

Paul advised the Philippians, "Let your conversation be as it becometh the gospel of Christ" (1:27, KJV). Our conversation—our speech—indicates the content of our life. Thus, Paul urged the Colossians, "Let your speech always be gracious, seasoned with salt" (4:6) and admonished the Ephesians, "Let no evil talk come out of your mouths, but only what is useful for building up, . . . so that your words may give grace to those who hear" (4:29). Most of us may not have experienced the dynamic potential of the conversation to which Paul calls the Philippians, but we need to be aware that life is found in communion with God and in conversation with others.

Speaking and listening with this sort of deep meaning is challenging. All of us have experiences that we cannot easily talk about. Genuinely listening to others and reflecting back what we have heard them say can help them think clearly and gain perspective. Listening, then, is an act of love. When we listen to someone, we say nonverbally: "I value you. You are important." When we listen in a way that makes a difference, we surrender ourselves to the other person, saying, "I will hear what you have to say and will receive you as I receive your words." When we speak in a way that makes a difference, we speak for the sake of others; thus we contribute to their understanding and wholeness.

SHARING TOGETHER

1. Ask if anyone would like to share something special that has happened during the past week or two connected with using this workbook.
2. Spend six to eight minutes discussing the two claims: *God's gifts to us are dependent upon our desire to receive them,* and *The Holy Spirit will not waste any of His gifts on people who have little or no interest in them.*
3. Invite two people to share an experience of *prevenient grace* (Reflecting and Recording, Day 2).
4. Spend a few minutes discussing how prayer has worked in our lives as both a duty and a gift.

5. Discuss why it is important to claim the fact that *prayer is God's idea*. How does this acknowledgment support your praying? Ask for any responses persons might have received in "conferencing" about this idea.
6. Take the next three statements in turn—inviting affirmation, doubt, questions. *(a) God cares what happens to us; (b) God hears us when we pray; (c) God answers us.*
7. Spend a few minutes discussing the statement *Confession is a prerequisite, not to God's forgiveness, but to our receiving God's forgiveness.* Is this a new thought? Do you agree? How is it true? Have you experienced this fact?
8. Spend the balance of your time discussing *naming and being named* as the dynamic of prayer.

PRAYING TOGETHER

Corporate prayer is one of the great blessings of the Christian community. We invite you to go deeper now, experimenting with the possibilities of prayer in a specific fashion. First pray aloud together your "Lord, I am coming" prayer (Ps. 27:8) that you have been praying the past few days.

Now, bow in silence and prayerful concern for the persons in your group. In your mind, picture each person—bringing to awareness what you know about that person as you have experienced him or her in your sharing together, and praying silently for each.

After this period of silence, the leader will name one by one each person in the group, inviting a volunteer to offer a verbal prayer after the person's name is called. The prayer may be brief—two or three sentences—or longer. Think of the person whose name is called. What concern or need has been shared tonight or in the past weeks that could be mentioned in prayer? You may want to express gratitude for the person's life and witness, the role he or she plays in the group, or that person's ministry in the community, possibly in a family situation. Someone may be seeking direction or confronting a crucial decision.

Call one group member's name and offer a verbal prayer for that person. Call another person's name and ask someone to pray for that person. Continue until all group members have been prayed for. Close with a brief prayer for blessing and guidance for each person during the coming week.

PRAYER AS SURRENDER

Day 1

LAYING OUR ISAAC DOWN

> When they came to the place that God had shown him, Abraham built an altar there and laid the wood in order. He bound his son Isaac, and laid him on the altar, on top of the wood. Then Abraham reached out his hand and took the knife to kill his son. But the angel of the Lord called to him from heaven, and said, "Abraham, Abraham!" And he said, "Here I am." He said, "Do not lay your hand on the boy or do anything to him; for now I know that you fear God, since you have not withheld your son, your only son, from me." (Genesis 22:9-12)

I was sharing keynote responsibilities with Christian author and speaker Carol Kent. She told the story of her only child, Jason, who had graduated at the top of his class at the U.S. Naval Academy and was happily married to a woman who had two beautiful daughters from a previous marriage. Jason had been an honor student with a background of achievement in academics and sports, a commitment to Christ, and a lifestyle that mirrored that commitment. Then, on the night of October 24, 1999, Karen and her husband, Gene, learned that Jason had been arrested for the murder of his wife's first husband. He was found guilty and sentenced to life in prison.

Carol recorded her heart-wrenching story in a moving book titled *When I Lay My Isaac Down*. You know immediately where the title comes from. Abraham's story had become her story.

What a dreadful moment for Abraham. The precious child God had given him and Sarah was to be sacrificed. The story sends shivers of horror up our spines. God said to Moses, "Take your son . . . and go to the region of Moriah. Sacrifice him there as a burnt offering" (Gen. 22:2, NIV). How could it be? Can you imagine how you would have received that word?

The matter-of-fact way that scripture records the story seems unbelievably insane. "When they came to the place that God had shown him, Abraham built an altar there and laid the wood in order. He bound his son Isaac, and laid him on the altar, on top of the wood. Then Abraham reached out his hand and took the knife to kill his son" (Gen. 22:9-10).

Few of us can plumb the depths of that pain. But most of us have had an Isaac to lay down: a loved one, a relationship, a circumstance, that we have had to place on an altar in surrender to God.

Surrender is the core dynamic of abiding in Christ. Jesus was quite clear about it: "Apart from me you can do nothing" (John 15:15). The relationship between the vine and the branches is not one of equality. The King James Version of John 15:2 says, "Every branch *in me*." The RSV renders it, "Every branch of *mine*." Both make it unquestionably clear: the branches belong to the vine. The relationship is primarily a call to self-surrender to the vine, to Jesus.

Surrender is the ultimate expression of prayer. Prayer is a lot of things. It is praise and thanksgiving, intercession and petition. It is confession and contemplation. It is communion, simply being with Christ, deliberately recognizing and cultivating awareness of his presence. But at the core, at what I call "point real," it is surrender. That's not all prayer is, but unless we discover and practice prayer as surrender, we will not experience the full potential and power of it.

REFLECTING AND RECORDING

Has there been an occasion in your life when you had an Isaac to lay down? Make enough notes about the experience to get it clearly in mind.

What other "Isaacs" in your life do you need to lay down? Perhaps it is one of the following:

- a child suffering from alcohol or substance abuse
- a fractured or seemingly hopeless relationship
- a failed career
- an economic disaster
- exhaustion from caring for a disabled family member

Name an "Isaac" or "Isaacs" you need to lay down.

Sometimes it helps to act out our commitments. Imagine yourself placing each of the "Isaacs" you have named in your hands. Look lovingly at them for a moment; then lift them above your head in surrender as an offering to the Lord.

Now pray this prayer.

All to Jesus I surrender; make me, Savior, wholly thine;
let me feel the Holy Spirit, truly know that thou art mine.

. . . .

All to Jesus I surrender; Lord, I give myself to thee;
fill me with thy love and power; let thy blessing fall on me.
(J. W. Van Deventer, "I Surrender All," in *The United Methodist Hymnal*, no. 354)

DURING THE DAY

The stanzas above are from the beloved hymn "I Surrender All." It is printed on page 203. Cut it out and take it with you as your prayer for the next few days. Seek to pray it two or three times each day, memorizing it as a lifelong prayer resource.

Day 2

THY WILL BE DONE

Our Father in heaven, hallowed be your name.
Your kingdom come.
Your will be done, on earth as it is in heaven.
Give us this day our daily bread
And forgive us our debts, as we have forgiven our debtors.
And do not bring us to the time of trial,
but rescue us from the evil one. (Matthew 6:9-13)

Let's pursue the idea that prayer is surrender in light of the most familiar of all prayers, the Lord's Prayer. Surrender lies at the heart of this prayer. "Your kingdom come. Your will be done."

The truth is that surrender lies at the heart of the Christian life. Jesus made that quite clear. He said, "If any of you wants to be my follower, you must turn from your selfish ways, take up your cross daily, and follow me" (Luke 9:23, NLT). It is not enough to have right belief, not even enough to have right belief and practices, if self-denial is missing. John Wesley preached a sermon on this issue, titled "Causes of the Inefficacy of Christianity" (Sermon 122). In that sermon he acknowledged that we could be faithful in belief and action and still be ineffective in our Christian discipleship. He explained that doctrine and discipline can be undermined by the lack of self-denial.

The surrender of self and self-will are requirements for abiding in Christ. One of the lessons we learn from the saints is that they did not seek ecstasy but surrender to God. They knew that in the Bible, *submission*, or *surrender*, is a love word, not a control word. It means letting another love, teach, and shape you. On the human level, the degree to which we submit to others is the degree to which we will experience their love. Regardless of how much love another person has for us, we cannot appropriate that love until we are open, vulnerable, and submissive.

The same is true in our relationship to God. There is no question of God's love and desire to bless us. However, because he has endowed us with the wondrous power of free will, the capacity of choosing and willing, he cannot force his love and blessedness upon us. In God's extravagant love for us, he has ordered life and his relationship to us to be dependent upon our response. We cannot fully receive and appropriate God's love until we are open, vulnerable, and submissive. Aware of our utter sinfulness, we cast ourselves upon his love to be saved. Acknowledging our utter weakness, we surrender ourselves to his love and are made strong.

Andrew Murray reminds us that abiding in Christ and having his words abide in us teaches us to pray in accordance with the will of God. Praying "Your will be done" keeps our self-will in perspective and under control. We bring our thoughts and desires "into captivity to the thoughts and wishes of Christ." We grow in likemindedness to Christ, and our will becomes "transformed into harmony with His" (*Andrew Murray on Prayer*, 100).

I read that word and recalled one of my most memorable experiences—a day spent with Anthony Bloom, the Russian Orthodox priest who wrote so helpfully on prayer and the contemplative life. He completely disarmed me by summing up his understanding of contemplative prayer with a nursery rhyme he had learned in the United States.

> There was an old owl who lived in an oak.
> The more he heard, the less he spoke.
> The less he spoke, the more he heard.
> Why can't we all be like that wise old bird?

Murray's words and Bloom's image make it sound so easy. We know it isn't. Though we acknowledge with our minds and often feel with our total being the presence of the indwelling Christ, and we know that the God of love is forever wooing us, obedience requires deliberate intention and disciplined will. We have to start where we are, using what little obedience we are capable of today, and continually practicing until obedience becomes the natural response of our life of surrender.

REFLECTING AND RECORDING

Write a sentence or two expressing what comes to mind when you hear this claim: "Prayer is surrender."

Ponder the claim that in the Bible, *submission*, or *surrender*, is a love word, not a control word. What does that mean in our personal relationships? in our relationship to Christ?

If we have to start where we are and continually practice until obedience becomes the natural response of our life of surrender, what are the *little obediences* you need to practice today? Write a brief prayer expressing your "little obedience" of surrender.

DURING THE DAY

As you share meals with family or friends, pray the Lord's Prayer aloud together this week.

Continue memorizing and praying the words of "I Surrender All."

Day 3

SURRENDER vs. RESIGNATION

> Having a High Priest over the house of God, let us draw near with a true heart in full assurance of faith, having our hearts sprinkled from an evil conscience and our bodies washed with pure water. Let us hold fast the confession of our hope without wavering, for He who promised is faithful. (Hebrews 10:21-23, NKJV)

The way we pray "Your will be done" makes all the difference. I believe that much of our praying of the Lord's Prayer is a distortion. It is not surrender but resignation.

Think about it. How often do we respond to our trying experiences and overwhelming circumstances, our pain and suffering, with resignation? They are beyond our comprehension, defy any rational explanation, so far beyond our understanding that we think our only response is to resign ourselves to them.

Resignation is not a Christian response. It is negative, and I believe, sinful. It is sinful because it is self-focused, not God-focused. Resignation is an expression of our self-will and keeps self on the throne. It is a form of stoicism.

There were two major streams of Greek philosophy at the time of Jesus: Stoicism and Epicureanism. Both provided a specific response to life situations. "Seek out those things that make life pleasurable," was the Epicurean response. Avoid those things that cause displeasure, "for tomorrow you die" anyway—and that's the end of it.

The Stoic response was a courageous fatalism, "Keep a stiff upper lip. Steel yourself against the circumstance and rise above it."

For the most part, Christians don't fall into the Epicurean pit. We know there is more to life than fulfilling pleasure. Subconsciously, though, we become stoics. We decide to bear our burdens bravely, and resign ourselves to bear the trouble and pain circumstances may bring.

Resignation is negative. If we resign, we forgo action and shut off the possibility of growth. True surrender is positive and can become the height of Christian faith and devotion.

A portion of my own spiritual pilgrimage will illustrate the difference between resignation and surrender. In 2001, I was the president of Asbury Theological Seminary. We had known six years of phenomenal growth, both in terms of student body and endowment growth, creative expression of mission and vision, and expansion of our outreach. We had developed a world-class faculty and established a second campus.

As an independent seminary, Asbury does not receive funds from denominations or church bodies. Thus we depend upon student tuition, individual contributions, and income from our endowment. With the scandals and failures of Enron and WorldCom and the plummeting stock market, our seminary lost two million dollars in annual budget income.

As president, I was responsible for our fiscal situation as well as all the rest. In that period of economic gloom that overshadowed all our planning and decision making, I found myself simply accepting the situation. I couldn't do anything about Enron and WorldCom and the stock market. Without any deliberate reflection, I moved into a state of stoic resignation.

But God confronted me. In my devotional reading one morning, I came to Hebrews 10:23. I was using the Contemporary English Version, and this was the translation of that verse: "We must hold tightly to the hope that we say is ours. After all, we can trust the one who made the agreement with us." The New King James Version renders it, "Let us hold fast the confession of our hope without wavering, for He who promised is faithful."

The word of the Lord came to me through that text. Our fear of the future dishonors God. Resignation to present circumstances is not Christian because it puts power in the circumstances, not in God. Surrender to the Lord is the Christian response because it acknowledges that we are not in control, and we must be totally dependent upon him. Through resignation, we fall into the trap in which too many of us are held captive: we trust Jesus with some things some of the time when we need to trust him with all things all the time.

REFLECTING AND RECORDING

Spend four or five minutes pondering the distinction between *resignation* and *surrender*. How is resignation negative, and how does it keep us in control, or our self-will on the throne?

What are the circumstances to which you have resigned, to which you are simply keeping a stiff upper lip, but are growing more bitter? Write a prayer of confession and surrender.

DURING THE DAY

Seek an opportunity for Christian conferencing today. Talk with someone about the fact that praying, "Thy will be done" needs to be an expression of *surrender*, not *resignation*.

Continue praying the Lord's Prayer daily with family and/or friends.

Day 4

CLAIMING GOD'S WILL

> After the death of Moses the servant of the Lord, the Lord spoke to Joshua son of Nun, Moses' assistant, saying, "My servant Moses is dead. Now proceed to cross the Jordan, you and all this people, into the land that I am giving to them, to the Israelites. Every place that the sole of your foot will tread upon I have given to you, as I promised to Moses. From the wilderness and the Lebanon as far as the great river, the river Euphrates, all the land of the Hittites, to the Great Sea in the west shall be your territory. No one shall be able to stand against you all the days of your life. As I was with Moses, so I will be with you: I will not fail you or forsake you." (Joshua 1:1-5).

The book of Joshua relates the story of Joshua and the people whom God called him to lead into the Promised Land. It is also a personal story of promise. Joshua models for us what it means to live in obedience to God and claim the promises that are ours as God's children. Our lives are full of discouragement. Temptation often gets the upper hand, and we cave in to the offer of immediate gratification and the easiest path. When suffering comes, we drown ourselves in excruciating "why" questions. Or, more commonly, we simply settle for a bland existence of getting on from day to day, without meaning, without joy, without a vibrant relationship with the One who is waiting to join us on our everyday journey.

The first five verses of Joshua, quoted above, contain two important lessons: (1) Claim God's will for your life, and (2) Claim God's presence and power for your daily living. Those two lessons have meaning to our theme of *prayer as surrender.*

Here was a new leader. Joshua's mentor, Moses, was dead; and Joshua now faced the greatest challenge of his life. He knew how difficult and stubborn the people of Israel were; yet he was to lead them into an unknown land. He receives his orders. Unlike Moses, who tried to give every excuse when the Lord called him, Joshua doesn't debate. Joshua simply obeys. The entire book of Joshua is about Joshua doing exactly what God told him to do.

Stay with God's word to Joshua. "Moses is dead!" The entire Israelite community knows that. Joshua certainly knows it. Why does God speak in this fashion, stating the obvious fact of which everyone is painfully aware? This is not just a statement of fact. It is God's way of stating an important truth. How that word must have rumbled around in Joshua's soul. It was a dramatic marker, a historic divide. *Moses is dead.* This is a new day, a new time, a new circumstance. All that is related to Moses is in the past. You must live your life, Joshua, with your back to the past."

"Moses is dead." It is essential to hear that word if we are going to claim God's will. Along with burying Moses, we must have some other funerals. There are things that will bury us if we do not bury them—resentment, guilt, self-hatred, remorse, the constant need to prove, neurotic fear, self-condemnation. There are things within us that must die if we are going to live. There are things that would undo us, that would cripple us, that would make us less than persons. This is the prayer of surrender: living with our backs to the past; memories of past sin and failure, even memories of past successes surrendered to God's gracious acceptance and love, in order to know God's will now and for the future. Paul takes it to its fullness, claiming it as the essence of what it means to be a Christian. "Anyone who belongs to Christ has become a new person. The old life is gone; a new life has begun!" (2 Cor. 5:17, NLT)

One of my most dramatic experiences of this dynamic of death and resurrection happened at a retreat for laypersons many years ago. One day, a sixty-six-year-old woman asked for an appointment with me. We met right after lunch and walked down beside a lake, sat down on an old log, and began to share. Before long the woman poured out a heartbreaking story. One of two children in her family, she was four years old when her brother was born. When the brother was four years old, he began having epileptic seizures, which grew worse and worse. This was in the day before drugs that could control epilepsy had been discovered. Also, at that time there was a stigma attached to epilepsy.

The family's whole attention began to center around the brother. All their energy, time, and love were focused on that young child with epilepsy. He died at age twenty-four, when his sister was twenty-eight. She never married; so after her parents died, she had no remaining family.

The woman became consumed with bitterness, because she felt life had passed her by. She began to blame her brother and parents although they had not acted intentionally and had no control over what had happened. Her bitterness turned into hatred. At the time when she should have been dating and marrying, and perhaps having children, her family's energy was somewhere else, and she felt victimized by it. Now, forty years later and twenty years after her parents' deaths, she was dying of bitterness and hatred.

She had to bury that bitterness and hatred. She had to allow the memory of that whole life situation to be healed. So, there on that log beside that lake, we had a funeral. She allowed that part of her to die, and she began to live with her back to the past.

Living with our backs to the past not only lifts the burdens of what has gone on before, but also allows us to begin where we are and be obedient to God *this day*. We may slip and stumble; we may even forget God and return to trusting in our own cleverness and strength. It does not help to spend time in self-accusations, blaming, and anguished regrets. Nor do we exercise obedience by gritting our teeth and claiming, "I will" or "I won't." Again, we must surrender. We don't *will* life through ourselves and our resources; we *claim* God's will.

REFLECTING AND RECORDING

Ponder this statement for a minute or two: Most of us prefer the hell of a predictable situation rather than risk the joy of an unpredictable one.

What does that say about claiming God's will?

How does the statement relate to the call to live with our backs to the past?

What two or three experiences, relationships, or failures in your past do you need to bury lest they bury you? Write a sentence or two naming and describing each, and then surrender them to the Lord so that you may claim God's will for your ongoing life.

DURING THE DAY

Did you find someone with whom to conference yesterday? If not, seek that opportunity today. Add to your conversation about resignation and surrender the fact that surrender means living with our backs to the past.

Continue your "I Surrender All" prayer.

Day 5

CLAIMING GOD'S PRESENCE AND POWER

> [Jesus prayed] "I ask not only on behalf of these, but also on behalf of those who will believe in me through their word, that they may all be one. As you, Father, are in me and I am in you, may they also be in us, so that the world may believe that you have sent me. . . . Righteous Father, the world does not know you, but I know you; and these know that you have sent me. I made your name known to them, and I will make it known, so that the love with which you have loved me may be in them, and I in them." (John 17:20-21, 25-26)

This prayer of Jesus is permeated with the notion of abiding in Christ. He prays for his future, as well as his contemporary, followers. Jesus wants his disciples to share in his glorified presence with the Father (see John 17:5). With death imminent, Jesus has finished his work and is ready to return to his glory with the Father. But he wants us to share the glory of his ongoing presence and, in a mysterious way that we may never understand, to know the presence and power of his ongoing presence in the world.

Yesterday we began a consideration of Joshua, the successor to Moses as the leader of Israel. In the first five verses that tell his story, there are two important lessons: (1) living with our backs to the past in order that we may claim God's will for our lives, and (2) claiming God's presence and power for our daily living. We considered the first one and now look at the second: How do we claim God's presence and power?

Jesus' prayer that we might be one with him has the guarantee of the presence and power that come from abiding in Christ. Long before, God had said to Joshua, "No one will be able to stand up against you all the days of your life. As I was with Moses, so I will be with you; I will never leave you nor forsake you" (Joshua 1:5, NIV). To mark the eternal significance of this promise of God, the writer of Hebrews quoted it. "Keep your lives free from the love of money, and be content with what you have; for he has said, 'I will never leave you or forsake you.' So we can say with confidence, 'The Lord is my helper; I will not be afraid'" (Heb. 13:5-6).

Prayer as surrender enables us to claim the presence and power of God for our daily living. I would not even hint that this is an easy accomplishment. As I write this, my wife, Jerry, and I have been working on prayer as surrender in a concrete way for several months. Our nation and the global economy are going through a devastating financial crisis. Apart from our guaranteed retirement account with the church and the seminary, everything Jerry and I have accumulated is threatened by the current economic crisis; much of it we have lost already. These are tough days for millions of people in our country. Jerry and I will be okay; we may not live quite in the fashion we had planned, but we will have enough resources to live on. We will not go hungry or without basic needs. This is not the case for millions of people in this nation and around the world.

But here's my point. Unconsciously and unintentionally, our lives become tied up with things that don't ultimately matter. We're unaware that we have become attached to a way of life that doesn't even leave room for questioning how independent we have become, how much in control we are, and how little we count on God's presence and power. Surrender is not a part of our practice of prayer.

Ironically, as I first began to work on this idea, I received a call from a friend whose son had overdosed, and they were not sure he would live. It's not always clear how desperately a person wants to take his life in situations like this. What we do know is such persons are desperate about life and death.

So claiming God's presence and power has not been an academic exercise for me during the past few weeks as I have wrestled with my own situation and as I have talked with these parents and their son. The parents have had to deal with the pain of a loved one feeling so desperate about life that he would risk the possibility of death. The son, now recovering, has to deal with the shame—but more deeply, with the issues that almost convinced him that life was not worth living.

The only way I can share with my friends is what I have discovered for myself as I have dealt with my own situation, though my situation has been far less dramatic. How do we claim the presence and power of God for our daily living?

First, we have to confess that we have lived as though *we* were in control. For all practical purposes, God's presence has had no operational meaning in our lives. We have shown little or no expression of need for God's presence and power. We must acknowledge that, confess it, and repent.

Second, we have to claim God's presence and power even when we don't feel it. This is where immersion in scripture is so important. God's Word is clear. "As I was with Moses, so I will be with you; I will never leave you nor forsake you"(Joshua 1:5, NIV).

That promise now has additional fulfillment and power connected with it. God sent his Son, Jesus, to convince us of God's love and saving power. When he was crucified, God raised him in order that he might be with us daily, always. Jesus made that clear—"I will send the Holy Spirit," he said, "who will be my spirit, present with you and giving you power."

REFLECTING AND RECORDING

Recall an experience in the past year when you most needed to feel God's presence and power—the loss of a loved one, the suicide of someone you know, economic distress, depression that caused you to question the value and meaning of your life, an accident or natural disaster that claimed the life of someone you know, the loss of a job. Make enough notes about that situation to get it clearly in mind.

Spend some time thinking about whether and how you experienced the presence and power of God, how you moved through the experience. Did you share it with others?

The two discoveries I have made out of my own experience, shared earlier, are recorded here. Spend some time reflecting on these in light of your own experience.

We have to confess that we have lived as though we were in control. When I reflected on my own life, I had to confess that for all practical purposes God's presence had no operational meaning in my life, and I repented. How do you respond to this in light of your own experience? How much expression of need for Christ's presence and power is seen in your life?

We have to claim God's presence and power even when we don't feel it. The psalmist teaches us here. "When my soul was embittered, when I was pricked in heart, I was stupid and ignorant; I was like a brute beast toward you. Nevertheless I am continually with you; you hold my right hand. . . . Whom have I in heaven but you?" (Ps. 73:21-23, 25).

Stay with this verse for a while. This psalm is a good example of supplication, which we considered on Day 5 of last week. In supplication we turn our whole being over to God, trusting in God's presence and power even when we don't feel it. Is there anything here in this notion that has relevance to your life right now?

DURING THE DAY

Do you know someone who needs to claim God's presence and power right now? Pray for that person as you move through the day, but also get in touch with him or her—by phone, mail, e-mail, or best, a personal visit sometime this week—and share what we have considered today on our workbook journey.

Day 6

SURRENDER OF THE MUNDANE

> Therefore I tell you, do not worry about your life, what you will eat or what you will drink, or about your body, what you will wear. Is not life more than food, and the body more than clothing? Look at the birds of the air; they neither sow nor reap nor gather into barns, and yet your heavenly Father feeds them. Are you not of more value than they? And can any of you by worrying add a single hour to your span of life? And why do you worry about clothing? Consider the lilies of the field, how they grow; they neither toil nor spin, yet I tell you, even Solomon in all his glory was not clothed like one of these. But if God so clothes the grass of the field, which is alive today and tomorrow is thrown into the oven, will he not much more clothe you—you of little faith? Therefore do not worry, saying, "What will we eat?" or "What will we drink?" or "What will we wear?" For it is the Gentiles who strive for all these things; and indeed your heavenly Father knows that you need all these things. But strive first for the kingdom of God and his righteousness, and all these things will be given to you as well.
>
> So do not worry about tomorrow, for tomorrow will bring worries of its own. Today's trouble is enough for today. (Matthew 6:25-34)

Yesterday we noted two essentials for claiming God's presence and power: (1) We have to confess that we have lived as though we were in control, and (2) we have to claim God's presence and power even when we don't feel it.

The second essential addresses us where most of us are most of the time. Our daily lives are alive with God's presence, but we don't "feel" his presence. That's the reason abiding in Christ as the way of living prayer requires cultivating *awareness of his presence.*

Kathleen Norris has been a helpful source and guide in my spiritual journey. I purchased one of her books because I knew her name but was puzzled by the title, *The Quotidian Mysteries*. I had never heard the word *quotidian* and was intrigued by such a strange word connected with mysteries. It sounded cultic and esoteric.

How surprised I was. *Quotidian* means daily or ordinary. In this book Norris shares the story of Brother Lawrence, who experienced the presence of Christ as vividly while washing pots and pans in the monastery as he did in the Blessed Sacrament of Holy Communion. "It is a quotidian mystery," she says, "that dailyness can lead to such despair and yet also be at the core of our salvation."

The surrender of the mundane, the dailyness of our lives, saves us from despair, enabling our daily ordinary rhythm to be redeemed and become the core of our salvation. Norris talks about this in terms of her vocation as a writer.

> I do detect in the quotidian . . . rhythms of writing a stage that might be described as parturient, or in labor, about to produce or come forth with an idea or discovery. And it always seems that just when daily life seems most unbearable, stretching out before me like a prison sentence, when I seem most dead inside, reduced to mindlessness, bitter tears or both, that what is inmost breaks forth, and I realize that what had seemed "dead time" was actually a period of gestation. (Norris, *The Quotidian Mysteries*, 10)

Prayer as surrender is the dynamic that makes the "dead time"—or any of our ordinary times—a seedbed where something new can grow or something dead within can be reborn.

REFLECTING AND RECORDING

Norris's word is a sobering one: "It is a quotidian mystery that dailyness can lead to such despair and yet also be at the core of our salvation."

Spend a few minutes pondering that thought in light of our reflection today. Is there a particular aspect of your life that is so routine that it threatens you with boredom, which you allow to pervade and define your whole life? Is there a particular ongoing mundane aspect of your life that you need to surrender to Christ?

Read again our beginning scripture passage. It is a part of Jesus' Sermon on the Mount, dealing with the daily concerns of our life that we need to surrender. Try to read it as though you have never seen or heard it before, and see if there is a fresh word in it for you.

Read the following prayer of Karl Rahner slowly, making it your prayer. After immersing yourself in it for two or three minutes, finish it with your own feelings and words.

I should like to bring the routine of my daily life before You, O Lord, to discuss the long days and tedious hours that are filled with everything else but You.

Look at this routine, O God of Mildness. Look upon us [humans], who are practically nothing else but routine.

DURING THE DAY

Give deliberate attention to your routine today. Seek to see Christ's presence in others, in relationships, circumstances, and events. Also be sensitive to the opportunity to surrender a particular aspect of your daily life that may not yet be surrendered to Christ.

Day 7

SURRENDER AND RESURRECTION

When they came to the place that God had shown him, Abraham built an altar there and laid the wood in order. He bound his son Isaac, and laid him on the altar, on top of the wood. Then Abraham reached out his hand and took the knife to kill his son. But the angel of the Lord called to him from heaven, and said, "Abraham, Abraham!" And [Abraham] said, "Here I am." [The angel] said, "Do not lay your hand on the boy or do anything to him; for now I know that you fear God, since you have not withheld your son, your only son, from me." And Abraham looked up and saw a ram, caught in a thicket by its horns. Abraham went and took the ram and offered it up as a burnt offering instead of his son. So Abraham called that place "The Lord will provide"; as it is said to this day, "On the mount of the Lord it shall be provided." (Genesis 22:9-14)

On Day 1, we considered the dynamic of laying our Isaac down. Recall that dynamic. Abraham's story is our story. In one way or another, at one time or another, to some degree or another, the time comes when we have to lay an Isaac down. It may be a loved one, perhaps a child who is wasting his/her life in the far country of alcohol or substance abuse. It may be a relationship, even our marriage, that is fractured—on the verge of breaking. We may be responsible for an elderly parent in a nursing home; the care demanded is wearing us down, and bitterness is creeping in. Or perhaps we lost our job because our company had to downsize, and we are hurt and angry because we were not treated fairly.

Surrender means we lay our Isaac down. "Thy will be done" becomes our ultimate yielding, not knowing how God is going to use our surrendered Isaac. We do know from the Abraham-Isaac story, but also from the whole of the Christian witness, that the dynamic of our life in Christ is death and resurrection. See it in Abraham's story. When he was about to do what the Lord had commanded him, offering his son as a sacrifice, the knife poised for the death blow, God interrupted. "Do not lay your hand on the boy or do anything to him."

What an interruption! And then came the affirmation, a central truth in the story. God said to Abraham, "You have proven yourself. I know how faithful you are, and how fearlessly you fear me. You didn't hesitate to lay your Isaac down, to lay him on the altar for me" (AP).

Can you imagine Abraham's relief? The heavy load was lifted. Abraham's heart was light, racing with joy-beats as he looked around and saw a ram caught by its horns in the thicket. I doubt if Abraham ever again experienced worship and sacrifice to the Lord like that, as he offered the ram the Lord had provided as the burnt offering in place of his dear son Isaac.

Prayer as surrender witnesses to the dynamic of death and resurrection.

Donald English, a challenging preacher and an outstanding New Testament scholar, once preached a sermon in which he invited us to imagine that we were tulip bulbs, comfortably tucked away in a wooden box on the garden store shelf—safe, dry, warm, very comfortable. One day a huge hand reaches down into the box and pulls out a handful of bulbs. The bulbs left behind say, "Whew! That was a close call! How fortunate we are; we have heard what will happen to those bulbs he took. The gardener will dig a hole in the ground and bury them. They will die down there, and earth will freeze over them. We're the fortunate ones. We're still safe and secure in our cozy little box."

In his inimitable way of preaching, Donald reminded us that spring would come; the snow would melt; moisture would penetrate the earth. Then the miracle of nature would happen: those bulbs that had been buried in the ground would spring forth in a spectacular expression of beauty—"tulipness"—that the other bulbs, safely tucked away in that box back in the garden store would never comprehend.

It's a challenging lesson about prayer as surrender. We have no specific notion as to how it is going to come out, but we know that the Lord is the Lord of the Resurrection. Easter is not just an annual experience. As we abide in Christ, and when we lay our Isaac down, when we surrender, praying "thy will be done," we can be confident that God will work his will and way for our good and his glory.

REFLECTING AND RECORDING

Read again the very first paragraph following the scripture passage above.

Go back to the "Reflecting and Recording" part of Day 1 of this week. Look at what you wrote and recall your prayer experience of that day. Repeat that exercise in light of what we have been considering all week—and with the added conviction that when we lay our Isaac down, when we surrender, resurrection begins to take place, and we can be confident that God will work his will and way for our good and his glory.

DURING THE DAY

If you are a part of a workbook group that will be meeting today, look back over the content and your reflecting and recording this week. Make some notes about what you want to make sure the group talks about.

Again today, give deliberate attention to your routine. Seek to see Christ's presence in others, in relationships, circumstances, and events. Also be sensitive to the opportunity to surrender a particular aspect of your daily life that may not yet be surrendered to Christ.

GROUP MEETING FOR WEEK FIVE

Two disciplines needed for abiding in Christ as living prayer are *intention* and *attention*. These disciplines are also necessary for meaningful group sharing. We must pay attention to what is going on around us.

In group settings the easy route is laziness. Individual group members may be tempted to "play it safe" and not risk honesty and vulnerability.

Energy is another issue. Listening and speaking demand physical and emotional energy. So the temptation is to hold back, to be only half-present, and to fail to invest the attention and focus essential for full participation.

I urge you to withstand these temptations. These sharing sessions are important. Don't underestimate the value of each person's contribution.

SHARING TOGETHER

1. Spend eight to ten minutes discussing the idea that prayer is surrender. Is this a new idea? How did you respond to it when you first read it? How does it fit into your understanding of prayer? Do you see *surrender* or *submission* as a "love" word, not a "control" word?
2. Invite two or three persons to share their experience of "laying an Isaac down."
3. Spend four to six minutes discussing the difference between *surrender* and *resignation.*
4. Ask if anyone would like to share an experience of moving from "resignation" to "surrender" in praying.
5. Spend a few minutes discussing the claim "Most of us prefer the hell of a predictable situation rather than risk the joy of an unpredictable one."
6. Invite as many as who will to share their experience of "living with our backs to the past" (Day 4). Urge those who will to share experiences of having to "bury" something, lest it bury them.
7. Discuss the two essentials necessary if we are to claim God's presence and power (Day 5); (a) confessing that we have lived as though we were in control, and (b) claiming God's presence and power even when we don't feel it. Invite persons to share their experience of either of these dynamics.
8. Invite someone to read aloud Karl Rahner's prayer on Day 6; then spend four to six minutes discussing "surrender of the mundane." Invite two or three people to share how they "finished" that prayer in their reflecting and recording time.
9. Discuss the idea that when we "lay our Isaac down"—surrender—resurrection takes place. Invite persons to share personal stories of this truth.

PRAYING TOGETHER

Sharing the prayers of our hearts with others not only confirms our prayerful desires, and claims but also inspires the prayers of others, adding the "two-or-three-agreeing" condition for answered prayer (Matt. 18:19-20). Spend time allowing those who are willing to offer brief prayers growing out of your sharing. As you begin, ask if anyone has specific prayer requests.

When as many as wish to have prayed, if someone in the group can lead in singing "I Surrender All," close your prayer time singing the two verses you have been praying this week.

AN INTERCESSORY LIFE

Day 1

THE INTERCESSOR OF OUR HEARTS

> Likewise the Spirit helps us in our weakness; for we do not know how to pray as we ought, but that very Spirit intercedes with sighs too deep for words. And God, who searches the heart, knows what is the mind of the Spirit, because the Spirit intercedes for the saints according to the will of God. (Romans 8:22-27)

On Day 7 of Week 2, we considered the Holy Spirit and the indwelling Christ, focusing on the difficulty of distinguishing, especially in Paul's writing, between the Holy Spirit within us and the indwelling Christ. Return and review that discussion now.

Our conclusion is that the New Testament makes it clear: There is no awareness of the presence of the risen Christ in us except through the Holy Spirit, and there can be no convincing validation of the claim that one has the Holy Spirit unless this is accompanied by signs of Jesus' presence. The Holy Spirit joins us to the risen Lord, and this relationship produces a life set apart for him. This leads to faith, hope, and love—and the greatest of these is love.

This understanding is important as we think more specifically and expansively about intercessory prayer. We can't think long about prayer without thinking about *intercession*. Though intercession is at the heart of prayer, often people who pray practice intercession the least and have trouble understanding and accepting it as a crucial role of every Christian.

Intercession is at the center of the Lord's Prayer: "Thy kingdom come, thy will be done on earth as it is in heaven." In one of his last recorded messages, Jesus centered on his concern and intercession for his followers and those who would believe in him because of them: "Protect them from the evil one. . . . Sanctify them in the truth. . . . As you have sent me into the world, so I have sent them. . . . I ask not only on behalf of these, but also on behalf of those who will believe in me through their word (John 17:15, 17, 20). The writer to the Hebrews describes Jesus as the Great High Priest "who ever liveth to make intercession" (7:25, KJV). In his instruction to Timothy about ministry, Paul wrote, "I urge that supplications, prayers, *intercessions*, and thanksgivings be made for everyone" (1 Tim. 2:1).

Verse 27 in the Romans passage just quoted is witness to intercession at the heart of our relationship to the Father, to the risen and reigning Christ, and to the Holy Spirit. Put that together with the fact that Christ "ever liveth to make intercession for us," and you have the dynamic work of the Trinity.

This passage from Romans (v. 27) pictures the Holy Spirit as the intercessor *in our hearts.* The risen Lord is our intercessor in the throne room of heaven. Here is the great mystery: as we abide in Christ, our intercession, the intercession of the Holy Spirit, and the intercession of the risen Lord in the throne room of heaven are one. This thought should fill us with at least a degree of awe.

David Chotka makes an affirmation about his understanding of Romans 8 and the prayer life of our risen Lord, who provides great clarification but also exciting challenge.

> It is now my settled conviction that when we are born of the Spirit something unique happens. We cease to be individuals living out private lives. Suddenly we become a part of the corporate body of the Risen Lord. We become physically and spiritually melded together with Christ as our Living head and we as His very body. His Spirit indwells us corporately together. We together, Christ as head and we as body, are the dwelling place in which God dwells by His Spirit. When something needs to happen on planet earth, Jesus prompts us by His Spirit to "pray it into existence." The groaning intercession of the Spirit in us is nothing more than Jesus' Spirit prompting us to pray into existence what needs to occur. God's Spirit and our dust join together. Through the agency of Jesus' Spirit praying through us, God *"causes all things to work together for good to those who love him, who are called according to his purpose . . ."*
>
> The prayer ministry of the church then is in fact, the very prayer life of our Lord. He intercedes for us in glory, and that works itself out by the Spirit of God interceding through the groaning intercessions of the Spirit filled church. The deeper our unity then, the deeper the intercession. The more we abide in Christ, the more we are able to receive the promptings of Christ communicated to us by His Spirit. (Chotka, e-mail to author, October 16, 2009, summarizing contents of *Power Praying*)

Again, unfathomable mystery is here, but it is a mystery we can claim boldly as Christians. We have been given the privilege of being connected intimately to God, primarily through our abiding in Christ. There is unspeakable joy in this privilege, but there is also the power to be used by God as instruments of making all persons his dwelling place, and all creation showing his glory. *Intercession* is one of the chief channels and means of grace through which the Father does his work in the world. The awesome fact is that *intercession*, unceasing intercession, opens the doors of heaven for the Father's blessings to flow and for persons to become partakers of those blessings. The intercession of God's people is a huge instrument in the coming of God's kingdom and the doing of God's will on earth as it is in heaven (Matt. 6:10).

Abiding in Christ, we find the confidence to pray with utter faith in God's power and willingness to do what we cannot do. Abiding in Christ, we are enabled to keep a rhythm in our intercession—a rhythm between persevering struggle ("moaning with groans too deep for words") and confident surrender. We must stay with our intercession with such faith and intensity that we demonstrate our confidence that we are heard by divine Love.

It is a stupendous reality that most Christians have yet to grasp

- that God rules the world through the prayers of his people
- that the expansion of God's kingdom is, to a large extent, dependent upon the faithfulness of God's people in prayer
- that God's ardent plea is for intercessors upon whom, by his grace, his work is dependent. Thus he waits for them.

REFLECTING AND RECORDING

Name two or three persons you have prayed for during the past few weeks.

____

____

____

In the space beside each name, make some notes about each person: his or her needs, what you prayed for, how long you prayed, what has happened as a result of your praying.

Other than persons, what causes—racial divisions in your community, the escalation of war in the world, the ongoing debate about health care, the diminishing influence of the Christian faith in the public arena—have you *interceded* for during the past few months? List some of these and make notes on how and for how long you prayed, whether other persons engaged in your intercession, and whether your intercession is part of an intentional ministry.

Does your recorded intercessory experience confirm what we have discussed about intercession in today's text? What is present? What is missing?

Read the following prayer several times; then in the space beside it, put it in your own words.

> Blessed Savior, strengthen my faith so much in the Father's tender love and kindness that my first instinct will be to go where I know the Father waits for me, and where prayer never can go unblessed. Let the thought that He knows my need before I ask, bring me, in great restfulness of faith, to trust that He will give what His child requires. O let the place of secret prayer become to me the most beloved spot on earth.
>
> I pray that you would everywhere bless the prayer closets of your believing people. . . . Lead them to regard prayer as the highest privilege of their life, a joy and a blessing.
>
> Bless especially the inner chambers of all your servants who are working for you, as the place where God's truth and God's grace are revealed to them, where they are daily anointed with fresh oil, where their strength is renewed, and the blessings are received in faith, with which they are to bless others. Amen.

DURING THE DAY

Find out if your congregation or faith community has an ongoing ministry of intercession, and if so, decide whether you want to be an intentional part of it.

Day 2

WHAT IF?

> Thus Solomon finished the house of the Lord and the king's house; all that Solomon had planned to do in the house of the Lord and in his own house he successfully accomplished. Then the Lord appeared to Solomon in the night and said to him: "I have heard your prayer, and have chosen this place for myself as a house of sacrifice. When I shut up the heavens so that there is no rain, or command the locust to devour the land, or send pestilence among my people, if my people who are called by my name humble themselves, pray, seek my face, and turn from their wicked ways, then I will hear from heaven, and will forgive their sin and heal their land." (2 Chronicles 7:11-14)

What if there are some things God either cannot or will not do until and unless people pray? For a long time now this question has been central to my thinking. I have written about it and seldom teach on prayer without introducing it. To even ask the question may be shocking to some, because it may appear that I am challenging the sovereignty and power of God. Think. It's commonplace for us to affirm that God acts through persons. God's will is accomplished through us, we say; and on earth his will and his work must be our own. Why is it such a mental leap to think that God may depend as much upon our praying as upon our acting?

It's a mystery. Yet scripture and Christian history offer convincing evidence that God is as dependent upon our praying as he is upon our acting. There's a marvelous story confirming this in Exodus 17, the story of Israel's first battle with the Amalekites at Rephidim. Joshua commanded the army of Israel, and Moses, Aaron, and Hur went up on the mountain to pray. Scripture tells us that when Moses lifted up his hands in prayer, Israel prevailed. When he lowered his hands, the Amalekites prevailed. So Aaron and Hur had to sustain Moses, to hold up his hands in prayer, and Israel was victorious. The soldiers on the battlefield alone could not make the difference; it also required the intercessors on the mountain.

The question is worthy of deliberate thought and response: *what if there are some things God either cannot or will not do until and unless people pray?*

God's promises to act in history and in our personal lives are often connected with conditions that we are to meet. The classic example of this in the Old Testament is this passage from 2 Chronicles 7: "If my people . . . will humble themselves and pray and seek my face and turn from their wicked ways . . ." Those are the conditions. The promise is, "Then will I hear from heaven and will forgive their sin and will heal their land" (v. 14, NIV).

The classic example in the New Testament is a part of the theme verses for this workbook journey. "If you abide in me, and my words abide in you, ask for whatever you wish, and it will be done for you" (John 15:7).

For reasons we may never understand, God has chosen to use prayer as an instrument of change, healing, redemption, and reconciliation. Here is a dramatic illustration of that truth.

Some time ago, one of our Asbury graduates, Jeannine Brabon, sent me a gift that I treasure. It is a wood carving of praying hands. It sits in my study as a reminder of the demanding and thrilling call to intercession. Jeannine is a missionary working in Medellín, Colombia. Her primary assignment is as an Old Testament professor in the seminary there, but her most exciting work is connected with the Bellavista prison. In 2009, the World Methodist Council gave her the World Methodist Peace Award for her work in this prison and reconciliation in that war-ravaged nation.

Bellavista has been one of the worst prisons in all of Latin America. It was built to house fifteen hundred inmates. Five thousand are packed into it like bundles of human flesh. Until a few years ago, it was a hell pit of violence and inhumanity—prisoners raping one another, heads cut off and kicked about like soccer balls, men hung up and quartered like hogs at the market, fifty homicides each month.

Then it happened. Oscar Osorio envisioned God wrapping the prison in his hands, and received divine orders to raise white flags outside cell blocks where prayer was taking place. David Miller's book, *The Lord of Bellavista*, tells the dramatic story. Prayer swept through the prison. Within six years, Christian conversion began to replace homicide. Where there had been fifty homicides per month, there has been only one per year since 1990 when Oscar Osorio and a band of Christians had their vision and responded. A secular jurist reported that violence in the prison diminished 90 percent. The warden and everyone recognized the power behind the transformation: prayer groups in every cell block.

My praying hands were carved by Carlos Velásquez, who was a prisoner in Bellavista and was converted as a result of the baptism of that prison in prayer. In his mind, they are the hands of Jesus. When you look at the carving, on the left hand you can see a black streak left by the lightning that struck the tree out of which it was carved. In her note to me, with this gift, Jeannine wrote, "There is nothing struck by disaster or devastated by sin that cannot be transformed by the Master's hands." Then she added, "The hands that carved these praying hands once processed cocaine for one of Colombia's biggest drug lords. Praise God. With him nothing is impossible."

Carlos spent ten days on our Asbury Seminary campus in March 2005, carving a larger-than-life Jesus as the "Good Shepherd" with a lamb over his shoulder. That carving resides in the lobby of the Student Commons at the seminary. Carlos not only witnesses with his art; he travels in the United States and throughout Latin America, witnessing to the Lord of Bellavista as the Lord of his life. He will tell you that through the dynamic of prayer, the Lord transformed his life and the life of that hellish prison.

The question demands the engagement of our minds. What if there are some things God either cannot or will not do until and unless people pray? But the question engages not only our minds but also *our wills*. If it is true—and scripture and Christian history say it is—then there is a more important question: What are we going to do about it?

REFLECTING AND RECORDING

Read again 2 Chronicles 7:11-14.

The following lessons are present in this passage from 2 Chronicles. Spend a bit of time reflecting on each of them. Make a few notes or write your questions beside each statement.

Prayer releases the grace of God.

Humility is absolutely essential—If my people will "humble themselves and pray. . . ."

Seeking God's face, a willingness to turn to God, is essential.

We cannot begin to discover God's will and receive his grace/favor without repentance and a willingness to turn from our sin and self-will.

The Hebrew idiom that underlies the phrase "in my name" refers to ownership. Israel was "God's own people." New Testament writers used that same terminology to refer to Christians (1 Pet. 2:9-10). Spend a few minutes thinking about how focusing on this truth of "who we are" should embolden our intercession.

Spend the balance of your time contemplating: If it is true that there are some things God either cannot or will not do until and unless people pray, what are we going to do about it?

DURING THE DAY

Engage two or three people today in conversation around the question, What if there are some things God either cannot or will not do until and unless people pray?

DAY 3

PARTNERING WITH CHRIST IN INTERCESSION

> Philip said to him, "Lord, show us the Father, and we will be satisfied." Jesus said to him, "Have I been with you all this time, Philip, and you still do not know me? Whoever has seen me has seen the Father. How can you say, 'Show us the Father'? Do you not believe that I am in the Father and the Father is in me? The words that I say to you I do not speak on my own; but the Father who dwells in me does his works. Believe me that I am in the Father and the Father is in me; but if you do not, then believe me because of the works themselves. Very truly, I tell you, the one who believes in me will also do the works that I do and, in fact, will do greater works than these, because I am going to the Father. I will do whatever you ask in my name, so that the Father may be glorified in the Son. If in my name you ask me for anything, I will do it." (John 14:8-14)

Three times in John 14, Jesus claims that he and the Father are one. First, in response to Thomas, Jesus makes the claim that is at the center of the Christian faith—not only is he *a* way but *the* way. He is the one, visible expression of the invisible Father.

Next, in response to Philip, Jesus presses his claim. "I am in the Father and the Father is in me . . . The words that I say to you I do not speak on my own; but the Father who dwells in me does his works" (vv. 8-10). Jesus' words and works are in fact the Father's.

Finally, Jesus repeats the claim of the mutual indwelling, "I am in the Father." Then he adds the claim that is the heart of our workbook journey, *"you in me, and I in you."*

In the context of that most important understanding, Jesus makes one of his most breathtaking statements: *"The one who believes in me will also do the works that I do and, in fact, will do greater works than these, because I am going to the Father"* (v. 12). Now here is a foundational truth for our understanding of prayer, especially intercession. After Jesus' ascension to the

Father, he will continue to do his works through his disciples *when asked to do so* (vv. 13-14).

One of the most challenging outflows of this truth is that we are partners with Christ in intercession. Jesus, aware of his coming death, prepares his disciples for the inevitable. He tells them that death will not be the end. He is going to the Father, and one day they will join him. In the meantime, Jesus ever lives to make intercession (Heb. 7:25).

Now, if Jesus is the "great intercessor" and has called us to do the work he has done, it follows that we are partners with him in intercession. Could it be that intercession is a big part of "the greater works than I have done will you do" that Jesus was talking about?

When I was leaving Christ Church to become president of Asbury Seminary, having been their pastor for twelve years, one of the gifts the congregation gave me was an enlarged reproduction of one of Charles Schulz's *Peanuts* cartoons, personally signed by Mr. Schulz. The congregation knew my fondness for Schulz's delightful but profound expression of theology.

Charlie Brown, always the "loser," is leaping with joy, dancing, and turning cartwheels as he comes to the door of his home, shouting, "I hit a home run in the ninth inning! I was the hero!" His sister, Sally, takes all the joy out his celebration with her incredulous "YOU?!"

Sometimes other people do the same to us—question any accomplishment or giftedness. But that is not our problem in living the Christian life. We, not others, are the problem. We will not claim the promise of Jesus, "Greater works than I have done will you do." We do not believe Jesus' offer, "I will do whatever you ask in my name." Jesus says that same thing twice in verses 13 and 14. He obviously wants us to believe it. Why do we so quickly settle for less than is promised and for so far less than is possible?

Abiding in Christ, we do not pray to someone far removed from us whom we have to convince. Rather, we join our minds, hearts, and wills with the One who is present within us \ in a mysterious way that we may never understand, the One who is with the Father, making the same intercession we are making. We are partners with Christ in intercession, so we pray,

- *having confidence before God.* "Let us hold fast to the confession of our hope without wavering, for he who has promised is faithful" (Heb. 10:23).
- *trusting God's faithfulness.* "[God] who calls you is faithful, and he will do this" (1 Thess. 5:24).
- *never doubting.* Jesus said, "Have faith in God. Truly I tell you, if you say to this mountain, 'Be taken up and thrown into the sea,' and if you do not doubt in your heart, but believe that what you say will come to pass, it will be done for you" (Mark 11:22-23).
- *boldly.* "Since, then, we have a great high priest . . . let us therefore approach the throne of grace with boldness, so that we may receive mercy and find grace to help in time of need" (Heb. 4:14, 16).
- *for the spirit of intercession.* "I appoint you to go and bear fruit, fruit that will last, so that the Father will give you whatever you ask him in my name" (John 15:16).

REFLECTING AND RECORDING

Spend some time reflecting on the notion that you are a partner with Christ in intercession. Question and test yourself in the role by examining the way you pray in light of the ways we should pray as partners in intercession, as we have listed those from scripture.

Having confidence before God

Trusting God's faithfulness

Never doubting

Boldly

For the spirit of intercession

Go back to your reflecting and recording on Day 1 of this week. Look at the persons and causes for which you have interceded over the past few weeks. Examine and compare the way you have interceded for those concerns to the way of praying we have discussed in this session. How might you change the way you pray in the future?

DURING THE DAY

If you have not engaged someone in the "what if" question we considered yesterday, do so today.

Is there a concern your group has talked about, or a person in your group for whom you need to intercede in a more intense way? Find occasions throughout the day to pray for that cause or persons, and pray that your entire group will have *the spirit of intercession.*

Day 4

AN INTERCESSORY LIFE

> You are the light of the world. A city built on a hill cannot be hid. No one after lighting a lamp puts it under the bushel basket, but on the lampstand, and it gives light to all in the house. In the same way, let your light shine before others, so that they may see your good works and give glory to your Father in heaven. (Matthew 5:13-16)

I was in South Africa a few years ago. The defeat and dissolution of apartheid was one of the most remarkable developments of the twentieth century. But that land is still a troubled one. It will take years to overcome the terrible fallout. Unemployment stands at nearly 40 percent. The AIDS pandemic tears at the nation's fabric, affecting every facet of the social and economic systems.

I found the church alive and well in spite of challenging circumstances. I was inspired by the commitment, perseverance, joyful worship, and compassion that are unabated by what seems an impossible situation. At every worship gathering, the congregants would light a candle and pray, "God bless Africa, guard her children, guide her leaders, and grant her peace."

Throughout the terrible and painful years, the Methodist Church played an influential role in opposing apartheid. Its members organized and acted, demonstrated and worked, and prayed. My friend Peter Storey was the bishop and longtime pastor of the Central Methodist Mission in downtown Johannesburg. On the altar in the sanctuary of that church was a large candle surrounded by a coil of barbed wire. It was beautiful and ghastly at the same time—a lovely candle with snarling wire biting out of it.

Every Sunday the people would pray for South Africa and the dismantling of apartheid. They read the names of those in prison for opposing the system and recommitted themselves to justice. Then they would light the candle. Suddenly, amidst those cruel coils of barbed wire, the light would come alive, and those Christians would remember the words of scripture: "The light shines on in the darkness, and the darkness has never put it out" (John 1:5, ISV).

That congregation knew and claimed its identity: a city set upon a hill that could not be hid. It is the witness of the church in South Africa, Eastern Europe and the former Soviet Union, China, and Cuba that prayer has been the sustaining power, giving courage, and, yes, transforming circumstances.

The life of the Christian is an intercessory life. The corporate life of a Christian congregation has the power of intercession. When we abide in Christ, prayer becomes our life and our life becomes our prayer. What Christ has been and done for us, we must be and do for others and for the world. On Day 5 of Week 3, we noted the truth that the branches do not sustain the life of the vine; rather, the vine sustains the branches. Yet, how thrilling and challenging—the vine cannot express itself except through the branches. Christ's expression of his life and work in the world is through us.

How have the presence and the love of Christ been most real to you? Has it not been through the love of others? To be sure, we must receive the forgiveness of Christ, but the dynamic of that forgiveness—especially for those who are being introduced to Christ and the kingdom community—is that they can begin to know that experience if they experience it with some other person or persons. So, in love, forgiveness, and acceptance, we make real the presence of Christ to others. Through us the working power of Christ in the past is brought into the present. Thérèse of Lisieux made this point in reference to Jesus' command that we are to love one another as he has loved us; thus his power is made real.

> Jesus, you never ask what is impossible. You know better than I do how frail and imperfect I am. You know I shall never love others as you have loved them, unless you love them yourself within me. It is because you desire to grant me this grace, that you give a new commandment. I cherish it dearly, since it proves to me that it is your will to love in me all those you tell me to love.
>
> When I show love towards others, I know that it is Jesus who is acting within me. The more closely I am united to him, the more dearly I love others.
>
> (*The Joy of the Saints*, 334)

REFLECTING AND RECORDING

In the space beside the quote, paraphrase Thérèse in your own words.

Have you heard anyone witness to prayer as a source of power, courage, and transforming circumstances in Cuba, Eastern Europe, China, or some other place? Call that witness to mind and spend a bit of time praying for that person and/or the country/situation involved.

Spend the balance of your time reflecting on how the presence of Christ has been made real to you—through others, through worship, through serving.

DURING THE DAY

As you move through the day, stay aware and act as though you know the truth of Thérèse of Lisieux's statement: *When I show love towards others, I know that it is Jesus who is acting in me.*

DAY 5

"I AM . . . YOU ARE THE LIGHT OF THE WORLD"

> When Jesus spoke again to the people, he said, "I am the light of the world. Whoever follows me will never walk in darkness, but will have the light of life." (John 8:12, NIV)

One of the striking features of the Gospel of John is the way it depicts Jesus' ministry. The other Gospels contain far more stories about Jesus. We read those stories and, like the disciples, we ask, "Who is this?" Who is this, that the wind and seas obey him? Who feeds the multitude on a few loaves and a couple of fish? Who makes the lame walk and the blind see?

The Gospel of John is different. It contains stories, yes, and clear accounts. There is never a doubt who Jesus is, because he tells us. One of the ways he does so is with statements that begin with the words "I am."

> "I am the bread of life. He who comes to me will never go hungry." (John 6:35, NIV)
>
> "I am the resurrection and the life. Those who believe in me, even though they die, will live." (11:25)
>
> "I am the vine, you are the branches. Those who abide in me and I in them bear much fruit, because apart from me you can do nothing." (15:5)

Today we focus on Jesus' claim "I am the light of the world. Whoever follows me will never walk in darkness but will have the light of life" (John 8:12).

This claim of Jesus blazes with meaning when we remember the context. Jesus was teaching in the Temple courts when teachers of the law and the Pharisees brought a woman caught in adultery. They stood her before the group as a humiliated wretch while they told Jesus about her sin. They rehearsed the law of Moses that called for stoning.

Wanting to trap Jesus, they asked him what they should do. My hunch is that Jesus looked them squarely in the eye, moving from one to another without saying a word. Then he knelt down and began to write in the sand. How unnerving for these self-righteous, stone-hearted religious leaders. They were certainly not ready for Jesus' response: "If any one of you is without sin, let him be the first to throw a stone at her" (John 8:7, NIV).

The silence must have been deafening. They had come so arrogantly, self-righteously, and boldly confident that they had Jesus in their grip. Scripture records their reaction in simple understatement: they began to go away "one at a time" (v. 9, NIV).

Law was the issue. What is right and wrong? How do we punish lawbreakers? But Jesus was saying that while *law* is important, *light* is more important. Law is good, but without light it can be cruel and oppressive.

Scripture compares Jesus to Moses; in fact, it refers to him as another Moses among us. That description is never in reference to Mount Sinai and the Law, but always as the deliverer, the one who leads us out of bondage. So, though Jesus insisted that he came to fulfill the law, he never called himself a lawgiver. What he claimed was, "I am the light of the world."

Now here is our challenge. Jesus said not only, "I am . . . ," but also, "You are the light of the world" (Matt. 5:14, emphasis added). This is radical. As Christ followers, we are what Jesus was and is—the light of the world.

When put together—"I am . . . *You are* the light of the world"—these words of Jesus form the platform for an intercessory life, a life of Christian discipleship.

Think about it. No Christian can evade the call and the responsibility. "You! You are the light of the world." There is no option here, no multiple-choice possibility.

Matt Friedman, a writer for a local paper in my home state, was part of a televised panel to discuss the problems plaguing Mississippi's capital city. The city was in disarray; the council president had been caught making shady deals with a strip club in relation to a rezoning ordinance. The panel moderator looked at Matt and asked, "Matt, whose fault is this?"

Matt said that suddenly he became agitated. He prepared to tell her in dramatic fashion that we are a nation of laws and that the council president had trampled on those laws. If blame was what we were looking for, there was only one place to put it—smack-dab in the lap of the council president as he sat in his well-deserved jail cell.

That's what he was going to say, but Matt never got the words out. One of the panelists sitting next to him was a man named John Perkins, author, teacher, community developer, and national evangelical urban ministry leader. Before Matt could respond, Perkins answered, "It's my fault."

Shocked, all heads on the panel turned his way. This is what they heard from John Perkins. "I have lived in this community for decades as a Bible teacher. I should have been able to create an environment where what our council president did would have been unthinkable because of my efforts. You want someone to blame? I'll take the blame."

Wow! How do you respond to that? What about the conditions in your community? What blame or credit can any one of us take for not being or for being "the light of the world"?

REFLECTING AND RECORDING

Name a person who you think lives out most fully Jesus' charge, "You are the light of the world": ____________________________. Make some notes about that person. What does he/she do? How does that person spend his/her time? How does he/she relate to others? How is he/she involved in a community of faith?

Spend a few minutes pondering this question: If my community's overall moral and ethical climate is declining rather than improving, where does the chief responsibility lie? Where am I in the picture?

Imagine the difference it would make if the 150 million people in America who call themselves Christians took this affirmation of Jesus to heart: "You are the light of the world." (Don't rush through this reflection.)

Does the congregation or Christian community of which you are a part see itself as the light of the world, "a city set on a hill"?

Reflect on Eugene Peterson's rendering of Matthew 5:14-16:

> Here's another way to put it: You're here to be light, bringing out the God-colors in the world. God is not a secret to be kept. We're going public with this, as public as a city on a hill. If I make you light-bearers, you don't think I'm going to hide you under a bucket, do you? I'm putting you on a light stand. Now that I've put you there on a hilltop, on a light stand—shine! Keep open house; be generous with your lives. (*The Message*)

Spend the balance of your time thinking about this call to you personally and to the Christian community of which you are a part.

DURING THE DAY

Continue seeking to stay aware and to act as though you believe Thérèse of Lisieux's statement "When I show love towards others, I know that it is Jesus who is acting in me."

DAY 6

RESPONSIBILITY FOR GOD

> Then the righteous will answer him, "Lord, when was it that we saw you hungry and gave you food, or thirsty and gave you something to drink? And when was it that we saw you a stranger and welcomed you, or naked and gave you clothing? And when was it that we saw you sick or in prison and visited you?" And the king will answer them, "'Truly I tell you, just as you did it to one of the least of these who are members of my family, you did it to me.'" (Matthew 25:37)

Jesus' parable of the judgment of the nations (Matt. 25:31-46) begins with the Son of Man coming in his glory, all the angels with him, with the nations gathered before him. He has come to judge, and he gives the basis for his judgment: "I was hungry and you gave me food, I was thirsty and you gave me something to drink, I was a stranger and you welcomed me, I was naked and you gave me clothing, I was sick and you took care of me, I was in prison and you visited me" (vv. 35-36). The "righteous" couldn't understand. When had they done this for Jesus? His answer was, "Just as you did it to one of the least of these . . . , you did it to me" (v. 40).

John Wesley taught that *works of mercy*, along with works of piety such as prayer, fasting and reading the scriptures, were a means of grace, a spiritual discipline by which we grow in

Christlikeness. For Wesley *works of mercy* were acts such as visiting prisoners, feeding the hungry, assisting strangers, and visiting the sick.

It is a sobering thought. How we respond to the "least of these" is our response to Christ.

When Dag Hammarskjöld was secretary general of the United Nations, on the eve of a meeting of the Security Council, he wrote to himself: "Your responsibility is indeed terrifying. If you fail, it is God, thanks to your having betrayed Him, who will fail mankind. You fancy you can be responsible to God, can you carry the responsibility *for* God?" (quoted in Paton, *Instrument of Thy Peace*, 13).

What an awesome, challenging question. It may be difficult to be responsible *to* God, but it is not difficult to think that is our calling as Christians. But how many of us have even begun to think in the fashion of Hammarskjöld—that we are responsible *for* God?

Alan Paton, best known for his novel *Cry, the Beloved Country*, was a white Anglican clergyman in South Africa, and one of the most outspoken and influential opponents of apartheid. He challenges us to think with Hammarskjöld about being responsible *for* God.

> I think . . . of a man who is leaving prison to return to the world. During these years he has paid more attention to religion than ever before in his life. As he leaves, the prison chaplain assures him the past is done, the past is forgiven. But when he returns to the world, he finds that the world has not forgiven, that it has not forgotten his past. So hope changes to despair, faith to doubt. It seems that God has not forgiven him after all.
>
> It is here that a great duty falls upon us all, to be the bearers of God's forgiveness, to be the instrument of his love, to be active in compassion. This man's return to the world is made tragic because *we were not there*. God moves in his own mysterious ways, but a great deal of the time he moves through us. And it is because we are not there that so many do not believe in God's love. (Ibid., 12–13)

We must never think or say we are not able or fit to be used by God. God can use us if we are willing to be used, no matter who we are or what our weaknesses may be. Maybe as difficult to believe is that God can use any other person who is willing, whatever his or her weakness. We have a dual challenge: (1) to be willing to let God use us, and (2) to assure others that they too can be used.

As Christ followers we are what Jesus was and is—the light of the world. As radical and as impossible as it appears to be, we can't escape from this fact. We must go where Jesus would go, do what Jesus would do, say what Jesus would say, and be what Jesus would be.

The saying attributed to Saint Francis of Assisi haunts me: "Preach the gospel at all times, and if necessary, use words." To be light may mean speaking, but it always involves more. We must go to, identify with, care for, love, and serve those with whom we want to share Christ.

My preacher daughter, Kim Reisman, made the case powerfully. In a blog on her Web page (nextstepevangelism.org), she shared a synopsis of the movie *The Motorcycle Diaries* and her response to it.

The movie is the story of Ernesto (Che) Guevara's life-shaping travels across South America as a young medical student. Toward the end of the film, Che and his friend Alberto are working at a leper colony. There's a river that separates the sick lepers from the healthy nuns and doctors and others who provide care. In the evenings Che looks out over the river at the dim lights shining in the huts of the lepers, and you can tell that the river has become the metaphor for all that he has experienced on his travels: the separation between sick and well, rich and poor, landed and dispossessed, powerful and powerless, accepted and cast out.

On his last night at the leper colony, they celebrate Che's birthday with a party on the "healthy" side of the river. Late in the evening, Che wanders out to the dock with Alberto and stands looking across the river. Suddenly he says, "I want to be on that side of the river."

After that synopsis, Kim commented, "As I sat in my basement, on my comfortable couch with my nice TV equipped with surround sound and all the entertainment trappings, Che's voice echoed in my ears. —' I want to be on *that* side of the river.' Actually it wasn't Che's voice really. It was Jesus'. 'I want to be on *that* side of the river.'"

As Christ followers, hearing Jesus say, "I want to be on that side of the river" shouldn't surprise us. Of course that's where he wants to be. That's what he was all about. He wasn't about hanging out on my side—the "healthy side," the side of the haves. He was interested in what was happening on the other side, the side where the sick lived, and the poor, and the suffering, and the disenfranchised, and the outcast. That's the good news of Jesus Christ. "I am . . . you are the light of the world." When we find ourselves on that side of the river—when we're suffering alone, when we feel marginalized or abandoned or confused or lonely or inadequate or lost, Jesus is there with us to comfort, to guide, to strengthen, to lift up. He meets us there. "I am the light of the world."

But more than this, when we go to the other side where the people who need Jesus are, we find him there. As Christ followers we are what Christ was and is. This is the nature of an intercessory life. "I am . . . you are the light of the world."

REFLECTING AND RECORDING

Following his reflection on God using us, Alan Paton offered this prayer:

To those who have lost their way, let me restore it to them.
To those who are aimless, let me bring purpose.
To those who do not know who they are, let me teach them that they are the children of God and can be used as His instruments in the never-ending work of healing and redemption.
(Paton, *Instrument of Thy Peace*, 16)

The prayer is for *those who have lost their way*. Name someone you know who seems to have lost his or her way. Pray for him or her.

those who are aimless. Name someone you know who seems aimless, without a sense of purpose or direction. Pray for him or her.

those who do not know who they are. Name someone who seems to be seeking for identity. Pray for him or her.

DURING THE DAY

Find a way to put your prayers into action today in relation to at least one of the persons for whom you have prayed. Call or write that individual. If you can help meet his or her material or physical needs, do so.

DAY 7

WHAT CHRIST HAS BEEN AND DONE FOR US

> A leper came to him beseeching him, and kneeling said to him, "If you will, you can make me clean." Moved with pity, [Jesus] stretched out his hand and touched him, and said to him, "I will; be clean." And immediately the leprosy left him, and he was made clean. (Mark 1:40-42, RSV)

Think about the scripture that has been our primary consideration during the past few days. In John's Gospel, Jesus leaves us with no doubt about who he is. He tells us. "I am the bread of life. I am the good shepherd. I am the door. I am the vine. I am the resurrection and the life." Using all sorts of images, he tells us who he is in wonderful "I am" claims.

He connects one of those claims, *"I am the light of the world,"* with who we are as his followers. *"I am . . . You are the light of the world."* As we abide in Christ, the light of the world, we become the light of the world.

Can you imagine how excited the disciples must have been, how overcome with joy they were, when they heard words from Jesus like these: "You are the light of the world" or "You are the salt of the earth"? Remember who they were, for the most part—not persons of social or economic standing, not persons being affirmed in their community, not persons with status or influence. Can you imagine the stirrings of their hearts, how their minds must have contorted as they wrestled with what they were hearing? Jesus was giving them a new sense of their value as persons; he was pronouncing an awesome word: you have significance in the world. A long time before, God had spoken directly to Moses, calling him to deliver his people from slavery. Moses offered excuse after excuse about his lack of qualifications. God assured him that his presence with him was enough. Israel's deliverance was not dependent upon human giftedness or strength but upon God's presence and power. But Moses continued his excuses by mentioning his inability to speak, begging God to send someone else.

God became angry. Moses was not the only instrument; there was his brother, Aaron. "I know that he can speak fluently," God said, "even now he is coming out to meet you. . . . You shall speak to him and put the words in his mouth; and I will be with your mouth and with his mouth, and will teach you what you shall do" (Exod. 4:14-17).

None of us is expected to do everything, but each of us is expected to do something for God. Humility is an essential Christian virtue, but it never allows us the opportunity to decline being used by the Lord. We are God's instruments.

Thus, it follows that *what Christ has been and done for us, we must be and do for others.* This is the platform for Christian discipleship.

As Christ has been a loving and affirming presence in our lives, so we must be a loving and affirming presence in the lives of others. As Christ has been a forgiving presence in our lives, so we must be a forgiving presence in the lives of others. As Christ has given us comfort and hope, so we must give comfort and hope to others. As Christ has walked with us through the valley of the shadow of death—guiding, sustaining, and encouraging—so we must walk with others through their darkest nights and most dangerous valleys.

One of my favorite New Testament stories is the one of Jesus healing a leper. Leprosy was the most dreaded of diseases in Jesus' time. Not only did its victims suffer physical debilitation but also mental and emotional pain and anguish. Lepers were forced to live alone; they had to wear special clothing so others could identify them and avoid them. Perhaps the most abysmal humiliation was that they were required by law to announce vocally their despicable condition: "Unclean! Unclean!"

Mark tells of one of these lepers coming boldly to Jesus, kneeling before him and appealing, "If you are willing, you can make me clean." Then there is packed into one beautiful sentence almost everything Jesus was and was about. "Filled with compassion," Mark says, "Jesus reached out his hand and touched the man. 'I am willing,' he said. 'Be clean!' (1:40-41, NIV).

Live with that encounter for just a moment to get the full impact. By law the leper had no right to even come close to Jesus, much less speak to him. The leper knew that despite his repulsive disease and grotesque appearance, Jesus would see him, really see him, and respond to him as a person, not as a maimed, disfigured piece of flesh. Notice Jesus' response: he listened, he looked at him, and he touched him—three action responses that no one else would dare make.

It's a graphic story, and we can't evade the challenge. If Jesus' ministry goes to the point of involving him with the poorest of the poor, the ugliest of the ugly, can there be any question? As his followers—light as he is light—what Christ has been and done for us, we must be and do for others.

That means no Christian can evade the call and the responsibility. Our being the light of the world is not optional. As Christ followers we are what Jesus was and is. As we considered on Day 4 of this week, Christ's expression of his life and work in the world is through us.

REFLECTING AND RECORDING

Spend three or four minutes reflecting on this: Christ has imposed an amazing limitation on himself—he has no hands but our hands, no voice but our voice, no feet but our feet, no ears but our ears.

Look at the following statements in light of the limitation Christ has placed on himself, and the responsibility he has given us. Put names, make notes, and offer prayer as you consider each area listed.

As Christ has been a loving and affirming presence in our lives, we must be a loving and affirming presence in the lives of others.

As Christ has been a forgiving presence in our lives, we must be a forgiving presence in the lives of others.

As Christ has given us comfort and hope, we must give comfort and hope to others.

As Christ has walked with us through the valley of the shadow of death, guiding, sustaining, encouraging, so we must walk with others through their darkest nights and most dangerous valleys.

DURING THE DAY

Today and during the next two or three days, if possible, contact the people you have noted in this exercise. Offer your encouragement, support, and any help you can provide.

GROUP MEETING FOR WEEK SIX

SHARING TOGETHER

You are approaching the end of this workbook venture. Only two more sessions remain, so your group may want to discuss its future. Would the group like to stay together for a longer time? Are there resources (books, recordings, periodicals) the group would like to use corporately?

This workbook is a sequel to *The Workbook of Living Prayer*. Some of you may not have yet used that book. My *Workbook on Becoming Alive in Christ* is a study of the concept of the indwelling Christ. The group may wish to choose either of those workbooks to continue with together.

There may be group members who would "seed" another group to use this workbook, each of the three inviting two or three to join a group to journey together. People will respond more readily to you, since you have already experienced the workbook. You may think of other ways to share this workbook with others. Or some of you may want to recruit and lead a group using either *The Workbook of Living Prayer* or *The Workbook on Becoming Alive in Christ.*

1. Open your sharing time by having a volunteer pray his or her version of Andrew Murray's prayer (Day 1).
2. Invite someone to read aloud Barnhouse's word quoted on Day 1. Spend eight to ten minutes discussing the roles of Father, Son, and Holy Spirit.
3. Take this discussion further by exploring the idea that we are partners with Christ in intercession. If Christ ever lives to make intercession, does it not follow that intercession will be a part of our life if we abide in Christ? And what does being "the people of God" add to this partnership?
4. Spend some time discussing the claim that God's promises to act in history and our personal lives are often connected with conditions that we are to meet.
5. Spend some time in honest personal sharing in response to this question: How might/must my prayer life change if it is true that there are some things God either cannot or will not do until and unless people pray?
6. Invite individuals to name and share their descriptions of the persons they named who live out most fully Jesus' charge, "You are the light of the world" (day 5). When individuals have shared about these persons, discuss what they teach us about living an intercessory life.

7. Discuss the difference between being *responsible to God* and *being responsible for God.* Is that a new thought? How should you describe yourself in being responsible to and/or responsible for God? Have you been exposed to this kind of teaching? Do you think it is consistent with scripture?
8. Spend the balance of your time discussing the claim "What Christ has been and done for us, we must be and do for others," in harmony with the limitation Christ has placed upon himself: he has no hands but our hands, no feet but our feet, no ears or eyes but ours, no voice but our voice.

PRAYING TOGETHER

In Week 4, Day 4, we discussed a simple guide to prayer in an acronym: ACTS (A—adoration; C—confession; T—thanksgiving; S—supplication). Let's use that guide for our closing prayer time.

It is usually easy in a corporate setting to offer prayers of adoration and thanksgiving, a bit more difficult to offer prayers of supplication (intercession on behalf of others and expressions of earnest desire for God's will in our life and the world), and far more difficult to pray confessionally. Hopefully, by now you feel "at home" in the group and safe enough to be more honest and risk more intimate sharing. Try it.

Invite a volunteer to offer a prayer of adoration and thanksgiving. Remember, we adore and praise God for who God is; in thanksgiving, we thank him for what he has done.

Now enter into a time of confession. Begin with a time of silence, with the leader guiding in this fashion:

1. In silence now, let us make our individual confessions as we consider the condition of our hearts. Do you have a hard heart? (Pause after each specific naming.)

   Are you hiding something from a loved one?

   Have you been deceitful this past week?

   Have you lied or cheated?

   Have you lusted . . . given attention to pornography?

   What about sins of omission . . . failure to be merciful . . . to speak the truth in love . . . to give a cup of cold water in Jesus' name?

2. Invite someone to close this time of confession with a brief verbal prayer, or as the leader do so.
3. Now enter into a time of supplication and intercession, inviting as many as will to offer three or four brief prayers—remembering the needs of persons in your group, but also situations and conditions in your community—and don't forget the larger world.

ABIDING

Day 1

PRAYING AND PRACTICING LOVING ATTENTION

> Moses was keeping the flock of his father-in-law Jethro, the priest of Midian; he led his flock beyond the wilderness, and came to Horeb, the mountain of God. There the angel of the Lord appeared to him in a flame of fire out of a bush; he looked, and the bush was blazing, yet it was not consumed. Then Moses said, "I must turn aside and look at this great sight, and see why the bush is not burned up." When the Lord saw that he had turned aside to see, God called to him out of the bush, "Moses, Moses!" And he said, "Here I am." (Exodus 3:1-6)

Nothing exciting was going on with Moses. He was walking along old, familiar paths. He had probably been there hundreds of times before. By chance, he lifted his eyes and beheld a rather strange sight on the mountainside. A bush seemed to be on fire. He watched it, expecting to see it crumble into gray ashes. But to his amazement, it kept burning but was "not burned up."

Don't let the burning bush that keeps on burning divert you from the core truth of the story. The lesson is in Moses' response to this strange sight: *"I must turn aside and look at this great sight, and see why the bush is not burned up."* It was then, when God had gotten Moses' attention, that God presented himself to Moses.

God has to get our attention before he can present himself to us, and the way he gets our attention is amazingly varied. He is always looking for that opportunity to present himself, which comes when we give him our attention, when we turn aside to see whatever "burning bush" is there. Recall the pungent expression of the poet:

> Earth's crammed with heaven
> And every common bush afire with God;
> But only he who sees, takes off his shoes,
> The rest sit round it and pluck blackberries.
> (Elizabeth Barrett Browning, "Aurora Leigh," *The Oxford Book of English Mystical Verse*, eds. D. H. S. Nicholson and A. H. E. Lee [Oxford: Clarendon Press, 1917; Bartleby.com, 2000, www.bartleby.com/236])

Moses was intentional in turning aside to see this phenomenal sight. In our commitment to abiding in Christ as the way of living prayer, Moses' action suggests an ongoing discipline: the discipline of *praying and practicing loving attention.*

In prayer, we give loving attention through meditation and contemplation. Many spiritual writers see these practices as synonymous. In either practice—meditation or contemplation—we put ourselves into the presence of God so that he can change and transform our attitudes, understandings, and behavior. If there is a distinction to be made, Joyce Huggett does it most clearly. "While the person meditating mutters and muses on God's word, the contemplative pays silent attention to Jesus, the living Word—the one who is central to their prayer" (Huggett, *Learning the Language of Prayer*, 42). This being true does not mean we do not practice both meditation and contemplation, especially as it relates to meditation on scripture.

There is no substitute for living with scripture. It is "God's breathed word." We read God's Word daily. When we come to a passage that *speaks* to us—or an inner nudging says, "Pay attention to this"—we stop reading and meditate on the words. We may, in silence, simply turn the words over and over in our minds, or even repeat them until what needs to happen happens—the words move from our minds to our hearts. The mind helps us understand what the words mean, allowing them a place in our hearts to make them a part of our being.

Our definition of "living prayer" emphasizes *recognizing* and *cultivating awareness* of the indwelling Christ. So in meditation and contemplation, we give loving attention to Christ. In our prayer time we acknowledge whatever tension is present—the source of worries, the pressure of what needs to be done, or some troublesome circumstance in our lives—whatever prevents us from *relaxing* in God's presence. We cannot give loving attention to Christ until we hand over the pressures of our lives to God. We respond to the invitation, "Cast all your anxiety on him, because he cares for you" (1 Pet. 5:7).

Having transferred our pressures, tensions, and burdens to the Lord, we wait in expectation to become aware of his presence and to receive his love.

But we are not only to do this in special times, such as a disciplined time of scripture study and prayer. We are also to *practice* loving attention to Christ in the daily walk of life. We will focus on this dimension tomorrow.

REFLECTING AND RECORDING

One of the lessons from Moses' burning-bush experience is that God has to get our attention before he presents himself to us. That experience may come in many ways: the mystery and miracle we feel with the birth of a child, a tragedy that shocks us and gets our attention about the fragility of life, a touch of good fortune that comes unexpectedly and unmerited. Think about your own faith journey. Recall an experience when God got your attention and presented himself to you. Describe that experience in enough detail to get the facts and feelings of it clearly in your mind.

Read again Joyce Huggett's distinction between meditation and contemplation. Do you accept that distinction? If you currently practice meditation and contemplation, think about how Huggett's distinction applies to how you are practicing these forms of prayer.

Read again the passage from Exodus 3. Spend some time meditating on this scripture. When the message has moved from the head to the heart, spend some time in contemplation—relaxing; transferring your pressures, tensions, and burdens to the Lord; and then giving God your loving attention. Spend at least three or four minutes with this exercise.

DURING THE DAY

Move through the day with an intentional eye for a "burning bush." It may be something mundane—a "common bush afire with God." Pay attention and turn aside to see.

Day 2

ABIDE IN LOVE

> God is love, and those who abide in love abide in God, and God abides in them. Love has been perfected among us in this: that we may have boldness on the day of judgment, because as he is, so are we in this world. There is no fear in love, but perfect love casts out fear; for fear has to do with punishment, and whoever fears has not reached perfection in love. We love because he first loved us. (1 John 4: 16*b*–19)

Dallas Willard sets the tone and underscores the theme of his important book, *Renovation of the Heart*, near the end of the first chapter.

> Often what human beings do is so horrible that we can be excused, perhaps, for thinking that all that matters is stopping it. But this is an evasion of the real horror: the heart from which the terrible actions come. In both cases, it is *who we are* in our thoughts, feelings, dispositions, and choices—in the inner life—that counts. Profound transformation there is the only thing that can definitely conquer outward evil. (Willard, *Renovation of the Heart*, 24)

Willard's book is the most complete treatment of this crucial theme I know. He lays a foundation for understanding the ruin and restoration of humanity, outlining the pattern of personal transformation—not as a formula but as a systematic process that we have the responsibility to undertake as intentional Christ followers.

The dynamic of this renovation, this personal transformation, is abiding in Christ. By coming to us, and forgiving us by his death on the cross, Christ restores our hearts to God. He then indwells us, and as we cultivate and respond to his indwelling, our hearts are "renovated."

Read 1 John 16*b*–19 again. When we read this, we realize why Jesus described his love before inviting us to abide in his love. "As the Father has loved me, so I have loved you." Love is the very being of God. It is not simply an attribute among other attributes; it is the very nature of God, the essence of who God is. Andrew Murray wrote, "When we gather together all the attributes of God—His infinity, His perfection, His immensity, His majesty, His omnipotence—and consider them but as the rays of the glory of his love, we still fail in forming any conception of what that love must be. It is a love that passes knowledge (Eph. 3:19)" (*Andrew Murray on Prayer*, 103).

Though "beyond knowledge," this love of the Father for his Son is the measure of Jesus' love for us. That should set out hearts on fire, even as it makes our minds a bit dizzy. Think about it; think about it and tremble. As the Father was with the Son before the creation of the world and humankind, that love relationship was in place. God's love is eternal. On the cross we see this love giving all and holding nothing back. That love is *unlimited* and *unchanging*.

Julian of Norwich, one of the "giants of the spiritual life," struggled for years with the question, "What was our Lord's meaning?" The answer came after years of struggling over particular circumstances and issues in her life. That which came uniquely to her is true in general for all of us. "*Would you know your Lord's meaning in this? . . . Know it well: love was the meaning*" (Keith Beasley-Topliffe, ed., *Encounter with God's Love*, 65).

Yesterday, we considered prayer as meditation and contemplation in which we give loving attention to Christ. As a last thought, I suggested that we practice loving attention in *prayer* and *practice*. Jesus' call to "abide in love" is a call to practice. To be sure, prayer and practice should not be separated. Abiding in Christ as living prayer means giving loving attention to Christ all the time. We seek to live as Jesus would live, knowing that "love was [his] meaning."

James T. Laney gives powerful witness to this. Laney, one of the most authentic Christian leaders I know, served as a missionary, pastor, theological professor, dean of a theological school, president of Emory University, and ambassador to Korea. In every vocational expression, his Christianity shone through. He confesses that it began when he and his wife, Berta, went as missionaries to Korea to work with university students. They were young and had energy, commitment, education, and a desire to serve nobly. "I wanted to be really committed," he said, "to do something more than the conventional. I took my family halfway around the world in order to do so." This was his testimony.

> When we arrived in Korea, we were put in a remote house that hadn't been lived in for years, without a telephone. It was on rutted dirt roads and hard to get to. We found that even though we'd had a year of intensive language study, nobody understood what we were saying. . . . In rapid succession we had a fire; everything we shipped over by boat . . . was robbed the first night of its arrival. Our oldest child almost died from a misdiagnosed case of scarlet fever. Berta, after having our daughter Mary, got the shingles. . . .
>
> We had arrived as confident Americans. Oh, we were dedicated, and we thought we knew what we were doing and we wanted to serve. We wanted to serve, but we were not really prepared to be servants. Do you understand the difference? We wanted to serve, but we wanted to serve on *our* terms, and we had all those terms taken away. We were divested of security. We were emotionally and physically depleted. We were no longer heroic.
>
> It was at that moment that God's grace intervened in the form of our dear Christian friends in Korea. They saw us now no longer as the set-apart Americans or the privileged Americans or the confident Americans. They now saw us not as one *of* them but one *with* them. That made all the difference! No, we hadn't really emptied ourselves (most of this was involuntary), but we were emptied. (James T. Laney, essay in *Courage to Bear Witness*, edited by L. Edward Phillips and Billy Vaughn, 46)

Laney then affirmed the power of servant leadership, which expresses itself most powerfully in practicing loving attention to Christ and abiding in his love.

REFLECTING AND RECORDING

Read again the beginning quote of Dallas Willard (page 157).

Do you agree with Willard? How do you respond to the notion that the primary "wrongness" in human life is not what we do . . . *but who we are*? How about the idea that the real "horror" is the heart from which horrible actions come? Ponder these claims.

Spend a few minutes thinking of some people you know who are like James Laney. Picture them in your mind, and relish thoughts about their life of love and self-giving, and then offer a prayer of thanksgiving for them.

Laney expressed what he believed was the secret of his effectiveness as a missionary: "They now saw us as not one *of* them but one *with* them." We keep telling ourselves that we must be one of them when we are thinking of those we wish to serve and witness to for Christ. Might we be wrong? Can we be one *of* them and still not be one *with* them?

In a stanza of one of his greatest hymns, Charles Wesley wrote:

> He left his Father's throne above (so free, so infinite his grace!),
> emptied himself of all but love,
> and bled for Adam's helpless race.
> (Wesley, "And Can It Be That I Should Gain, no. 363, *The United Methodist Hymnal*)

Write a few sentences describing what it would mean for you to "empty yourself of all but love."

DURING THE DAY

Contact at least one of the persons you thought of and prayed for earlier, and thank that individual for his or her service and witness.

Day 3

OBEDIENCE THROUGH ABIDING

[Jesus said] "If you love me, you will keep my commandments. And I will ask the Father, and he will give you another Advocate, to be with you forever. This is the Spirit of truth, whom the world cannot receive, because it neither sees him nor knows him. You know him, because he abides with you, and he will be in you. . . .

Jesus answered [Judas, not Iscariot], "Those who love me will keep my word, and my Father will love them, and we will come to them and make our home with them. Whoever does not love me does not keep my words; and the word that you hear is not mine, but is from the Father who sent me." (John 14:15-17, 23-24)

Throughout this workbook journey, we have talked a lot about love. We have concentrated specifically on love the past two days. Love is such an easy word to say, yet such a difficult thing to do. In our Christian walk, we must come to the place where we realize that ultimately love shows itself not in our declarations of affection but in how we relate to those we profess to love. This is obviously true in human relationships. To love another means we move beyond verbal expression of our feelings to acts of caring, acts that inconvenience us and may even be sacrificial. This is certainly true in our relationship to Christ. Jesus was clear about it: "If you love me, you will keep my commandments" (John 14:15). In the next chapter he says it this way: "If you keep my commandments, you will abide in my love, just as I have kept my Father's commandments and abide in his love"(15:10). Obedience is connected with—in fact, made possible through—abiding in Christ. The surrender of self-will comes through abiding.

For many years I have practiced what I call "keeping company with the saints." Throughout the ages many persons have diligently sought God and committed to living in as intimate a relationship with him as possible. I learned from reading and "keeping company" with these persons that they shared ten common characteristics. The first two of those traits were that they passionately sought the Lord and discovered a gracious God. Another characteristic was that they were convinced that obedience was essential to their life and growth. (Dunnam, *The Workbook on Lessons from the Saints*, 3). .

We have a right to ask, to seek, and to know the will of God, but once we know it, nothing but obedience will do. Learning and living obedience through abiding in Christ brings us to the place where the primary longing of our life is to walk in a way that will please God and bring glory to God's name.

Our spiritual formation is a dynamic process, a growing willingness, even a willingness to be made willing, to say yes to God each day in every way possible—no matter what the circumstances. By abiding in Christ, we pay attention to God, and the more attention we pay to God, the more aware we become of the yet-to-be-redeemed areas of our life. Thus, the more aware we are of our need to surrender ourselves to the transforming power of the indwelling Christ.

Obedience comes through abiding, because when we abide in Christ, our self-will is diminished. In Christ we discover that obedience means abandoning ourselves to God. Only in the confidence that is ours in our awareness of the presence of Christ can we abandon ourselves to God. The closer we are to Christ, the more aware we are of his presence, and the less fear we have of responding to God's call.

Consider what this does for our *praying*. Abiding in Christ, and having his words abide in us, guides us to pray in accordance to God's will. If we are not living in obedience, we have at least mental reservations about claiming Jesus' promise, "Whatever you ask in my name I will do it." We certainly have "faith reservations" if we are not obedient. How can we ask "in Jesus' name" if we are not being faithful and obedient to Jesus' name?

If we are obedient, which comes and is sustained in our abiding, we can pray boldly because we are abandoned to God and are verifying our longing to walk in a way that will please him and bring glory to his name.

Consider also how our obedience *shapes how we serve and relate to others*. In the testimony of James Laney that you read yesterday, he said that his and his wife's work in Korea dramatically changed when "they saw us as not one *of* them but one *with* them." Obedience to Christ means we are abiding in his love. This necessarily shapes how we serve and relate to others.

Return to the notion that *obedience means abandoning ourselves to God*. It is through our abiding in Christ that such abandonment is possible. Jean-Pierre de Caussade, one of the saints who believed that obedience was essential for the spiritual life and growth, advised those with whom he counseled that abandonment to God "is, of all practices, the most divine." He wrote this word to someone who depended upon his spiritual guidance:

> Your way of acting in times of trouble and distress gives me great pleasure. To be submissive, to abandon yourself entirely without reserve, to be content with being discontented for as long as God wills or permits, will make you advance more in one day than you would in a hundred days spent in sweetness and consolation.
>
> Your total abandonment to God, practised in a spirit of confidence, and of union with Jesus Christ doing always the will of his Father, is, of all practices, the most divine. (Robert Llewlyn, ed., *The Joy of the Saints*, 101)

Paul's description of Jesus gives us a way to think about obedience.

> Let each of you look not to your own interests, but to the interests of others. Let the same mind be in you that was in Christ Jesus,
> who, though he was in the form of God,
> did not regard equality with God
> as something to be exploited,
> but emptied himself,
> taking the form of a slave,
> being born in human likeness.
> And being found in human form,
> he humbled himself
> and became obedient to the point of death—
> even death on a cross.
>
> Therefore God also highly exalted him
> and gave him the name
> that is above every name,
> so that at the name of Jesus
> every knee should bend,
> in heaven and on earth and under the earth,
> and every tongue should confess
> that Jesus Christ is Lord,
> to the glory of God the Father. (Phil. 2:4-11)

REFLECTING AND RECORDING

Spend a couple of minutes reflecting on this statement: We have a right to ask, to seek, and to know the will of God, but once we know it, nothing but obedience will do.

Our claim is that by abiding in Christ, we pay attention to God, and the more attention we pay to God, the more we become aware of the yet-to-be-redeemed areas of our life. Thus the more we need to surrender ourselves to the transforming power of the indwelling Christ. We've been on this workbook journey for six weeks now, and we've been paying attention to our spiritual state. Have you discovered any yet-to-be-redeemed areas of your life? Ponder that and make some notes here, and in prayer, surrender what you discover.

Now spend a couple of minutes considering whether and how obedience shapes your praying. When you are earnestly seeking and doing God's will, are your prayers freer, bolder, more confident? Is there any resistance to God's will in your life right now that might be affecting the way you pray?

What does Jean-Pierre de Caussade's phrase "to be content with being discontented" mean? Have you experienced discontentment that God may have wanted you to be "content with"? In what way has discontentment been a source of spiritual growth? Spend a few minutes reflecting on this issue.

DURING THE DAY

Surrender is a disposition that comes from the *will*. Make the disposition of surrender your aim for the next five days.

Day 4

THE EXPULSIVE POWER OF A NEW AFFECTION

With this in mind, then, I kneel in prayer to the Father, from whom every family in heaven and on earth takes its name, that out of the treasures of his glory he may grant you strength and power through his Spirit in your inner being, that through faith Christ may dwell in your hearts in love. With deep roots and firm foundations, may you be strong to grasp, with all God's people, what is the breadth and length and height and depth of the love of Christ, and to know it, though it is beyond knowledge. So may you attain to fullness of being, the fullness of God himself. (Ephesians 3:14-19, NEB)

In the deep heart
of [humans] was a shrine where none but
God was worthy to come. Within [the human
heart] was God; without, a thousand gifts
which God had showered upon [humanity].
[Sin] made those very gifts of God a potential
source of ruin to the soul.

Our woes began when God was forced out of
His central shrine and things were allowed to enter.
Within the human heart things have taken over.
[People] have now by nature no peace within their
hearts, for God is crowned there no longer,
but there in the moral dusk stubborn and
aggressive usurpers fight among themselves
for first place on the throne.
(Tozer, *The Pursuit of God*, 21–22)

This is an accurate analysis of the human condition. It is the primary way sin expresses itself in our lives—*the nature to possess. Me, my,* and *mine* are common words in our vocabulary. Tiny words, and innocent-looking in print, they describe the spiritual disease that spells our death. Possessions—things—have become essential; we think we can't live without them. Everything that God intended as gifts has become idols.

It isn't the "bad" things we do that spell spiritual dryness or even ruin for most of us but the good things that become overly important. Possessions begin to dominate who we are and how we respond to situations and to others. It is so easy to get excited about what we are doing or what is ours that we become guilty of idolatry; we worship ourselves and things rather than the Lord. Idolatry means putting ourselves in control rather than God. We think more of ourselves and trust ourselves more than God.

The things that dominate our lives take different shape and expression: success, security, acceptance, image or social position, material wealth, style, and appearance. How do we deal with this deadly spiritual disease?

Thomas Chalmers (1780–1847), a Scottish mathematician and preacher, is the author of one of history's most popular sermons, "The Expulsive Power of a New Affection." He made the case that the heart is so constituted that the only way to dispossess it of an old affection is by the expulsive power of a new one.

With that thought in mind, read again our beginning passage from Ephesians.

These words leave us breathless—speechless. The last sentence alone is a spiritual/mental lambaste. "So may you attain to fullness of being, the fullness of God himself." What could be more mind-boggling, unbelievable, extravagant, and radical?

"Fullness of being, the fullness of God himself," is ours through Christ who indwells us. As we recognize and cultivate awareness of the indwelling Christ, we unleash the most effective "expulsive power of a new affection." What can have more expulsive power than being filled with all the "fullness of God"? Abiding in Christ as living prayer is the most powerful expulsive power available to us.

I don't know a bolder testimony than that of Paul. "It is no longer I who live, but it is Christ who lives in me" (Gal. 2:20).

This may be a good way to think about Jesus' word concerning pruning. "Every branch of mine that bears no fruit, he takes away, and every branch that does bear fruit he prunes, that it may bear more fruit" (John 15:2, RSV). The Greek word for pruning is *kathairó* (from *katharos*). It also means "to cleanse or purge." This is the root of our word *catharsis*, which means the relieving of emotional tensions, frustrations, and despair. So it is a conversion of the mind and renewal of imagination. Abiding in Christ, having his mind in us, has that converting, renewing power. We will pursue this thought tomorrow.

REFLECTING AND RECORDING

Read again A.W. Tozer's words. We need to understand the vital insight that everything that God prepared in creation for humans' use and pleasure was meant to be external and subservient to God. In the space provided on page 164, write in your own words what he is saying.

How do you respond to this statement: "It isn't the 'bad' things we do that spell spiritual dryness or even ruin for most of us but the good things that become overly important?" Do you agree? Have you experienced spiritual dryness because of allowing good things to become too important? Have you experienced, or do you know someone who has experienced, "ruin" because of this? Spend some time pondering this issue.

Be specific and name some "good things" that threaten to dominate your life.

Spend a bit of time now considering how being "filled with all the fullness of God" may be the expulsive power of a new affection for you. How might *abiding in Christ* be a kind of pruning dynamic?

DURING THE DAY

Remember, you are seeking, by an ongoing act of your will, to develop a disposition of surrender.

As you move through this day, notice what you consider most important and valuable. Ask yourself how your awareness of and dependency on Christ are being affected by how you value things.

Day 5

MAKING SIN POWERLESS

> His divine power has given us everything needed for life and godliness, through the knowledge of him who called us by his own glory and goodness. Thus he has given us, through these things, his precious and very great promises, so that through them you may escape from the corruption that is in the world because of lust, and may become participants in the divine nature. For this very reason, you must make every effort to support your faith with goodness, and goodness with knowledge, and knowledge with self-control, and self-control with endurance, and endurance with godliness, and godliness with mutual affection, and mutual affection with love. For if these things are yours and are increasing among you, they keep you from being ineffective and unfruitful in the knowledge of our Lord Jesus Christ. For anyone who lacks these things is short-sighted and blind, and is forgetful of the cleansing of past sins. (2 Peter 1:3-9)

Yesterday we considered being "filled with all the fullness of God" as the *expulsive power of a new affection.* "Fullness of being, the fullness of God himself" is ours through the indwelling Christ. Abiding in Christ as living prayer is the most powerful expulsive power available to us.

On Day 5 of Week 5 we considered the fact that we live as though we were in control, and show little or no expression of the need for God's presence and power. Yesterday we recognized that this is idolatry. Idolatry *means that we place ourselves in control rather than God. We think more of ourselves and we trust ourselves more than God.* This leads not only to dryness of spirit but even to spiritual ruin. So we need pruning, the expulsive power of a new affection.

As we abide in Christ, we are *pruned.* In vineyard language, dying branches and unproductive branches are cut off the vine and cast away—all for the purpose of our cleansing and perfecting, in order that we might be fruitful.

The New Testament is full of language about "putting off the old and putting on the new."

- Do not lie to one another, seeing that you have stripped off the old self with its practices and have clothed yourselves with the new self, which is being renewed in knowledge according to the image of its creator (Col. 3:9-10).
- We know that our old self was crucified with him so that the body of sin might be destroyed, and we might no longer be enslaved to sin (Rom. 6:6).
- You were taught to put away your former way of life, your old self, corrupt and deluded by its lusts, and to be renewed in the spirit of your minds, and to clothe yourselves with the new self, created according to the likeness of God in true righteousness and holiness (Eph. 4:22-24.)

Paul defines a Christian as a "new creation: everything old has passed away; . . . everything has become new!" (2 Cor. 5:17). The revolutionary truth of the Christian faith is that just as we have been *formed* by all the forces in human life, relationships, and circumstances, so we can be *transformed* by Christ.

The greatest barrier to the full expression of the Christian faith and way is the all-too-prevalent notion that we are victims of our human nature, thus not only prone to sin but unable *not* to sin. This is not the biblical message. We allow our minds to rationalize that we will always be slaves of sin. This is a deceitful lie of Satan. The role of spiritual disciplines, and the dynamic of abiding in Christ, is to put to death that lie and make sin powerless in its control of our lives. Sin dwells in our choices—our wills, and our wills can be transformed. The revolution of Christ is a revolution of character. We can indeed become "new creatures in Christ Jesus."

Read again slowly and reflectively the passage from Second Peter. Read it as though you were hearing a message for the first time. What is the passage saying to you?

Did you notice? Peter started out with a foundational truth: God's power provides us everything we need "for life and godliness." He sketches the basis of faithful living, identifying the Christian life as one of growth in godliness. It is an extravagant word. God has "given us . . . his precious and very great promises [that we] . . . may *escape* from . . . corruption . . . and may become participants of the divine nature"(italics mine).

The way of escape is laid out. "Make every effort to support your faith with goodness, and goodness with knowledge, and knowledge with self-control, and self-control with endurance, and endurance with godliness, and godliness with mutual affection, and mutual affection with love." All the disciplines of spiritual formation are called for. These disciplines are simply to undergird us in doing what is right and good, and to transform us into Christlikeness.

We Christians are so accustomed to thinking that sinning daily is inevitable that we do not even entertain the notion that by abiding in Christ we can make sin powerless. This happens not by engaging the mind every moment and being preoccupied with "how well we are doing as Christ followers," but by entrusting ourselves to the Spirit to provide us all we need. The psalmist said, "The Lord will keep you from all evil; he will keep your life" (Ps. 121:7). Since the psalmist's time, we have been given the glorious opportunity of abiding in Christ. Abiding in him makes sin powerless in controlling our lives.

REFLECTING AND RECORDING

What is your initial honest response to the claim that the greatest barrier to the full expression of the Christian faith and way is the all-too-prevalent notion that we are victims of our human nature, and thus not only prone to sin, but unable to not sin? This is a huge issue; don't leave your reflection too quickly.

Read again the passages of scripture printed on page 167.

What do these passages say about whether or not we are destined to be "slaves of sin"?

Spend the balance of your time thinking about sin in your life. Does it have control? Are you a slave to sin? Do you feel you are a victim of your human nature, thus destined to sin? Do you believe that God's power provides everything we need "for life and godliness"—that the indwelling Christ makes sin powerless in controlling us?

DURING THE DAY

Don't forget you are working on cultivating a disposition of surrender.

Sin dwells in our wills, our choices and decisions. We may sin, but we don't *have* to sin. Decide now that you will cease the practice of a habit you believe is destructive, hampering your ongoing relationship to Christ; that you will practice saying no to any negative temptation that portends sin gaining a foothold in your life.

Day 6

From One Degree of Glory to Another

> Since, then, we have such a hope, we act with great boldness, not like Moses, who put a veil over his face to keep the people of Israel from gazing at the end of the glory that was being set aside. But their minds were hardened. Indeed, to this very day, when they hear the reading of the old covenant, that same veil is still there, since only in Christ is it set aside. Indeed, to this very day whenever Moses is read, a veil lies over their minds; but when one turns to the Lord, the veil is removed. Now the Lord is the Spirit, and where the Spirit of the Lord is, there is freedom. And all of us, with unveiled faces, seeing the glory of the Lord as though reflected in a mirror, are being transformed into the same image from one degree of glory to another; for this comes from the Lord, the Spirit. (2 Corinthians 3:12-18)

In this scripture passage, Paul refers to Moses putting a veil over his face because he had been talking to God, and his countenance was ablaze in light (Exod. 34:29-35). In verses 10 and 11 of this same chapter, Paul says, "What once had glory has lost its glory because of the greater glory; for if what was set aside came through glory, much more has the permanent come in glory!" Paul is talking about the glory of Christ. This glory is now available to all persons. Abiding in Christ, we are transformed from one degree of glory to another. This is the dynamic process of *sanctification*.

That word, *sanctification*, has been placed on an almost forgotten shelf of the vocabulary of the church. Rarely do we hear that word in our day, in sermons or Sunday school. Though grossly ignored, it is a core dynamic in the Christian faith and way. It is certainly a central doctrine in the Wesleyan understanding of Christianity.

On Day 2 of Week 4, we talked about John Wesley's expression of grace working in our life in three expressions: *prevenient, justifying,* and *sanctifying grace.* Prevenient grace is the grace "that goes before." Before any conscious personal experience of divine grace, grace is present, working in our lives even before we are aware of it. Justifying grace is "saving" grace. When we respond in faith to God's grace, we are justified, or "made right with God," not because of our merit, but by divine grace. Wesley described this as "knowing our sins forgiven."

To picture the idea of salvation, Wesley used the interesting image of a house. Prevenient grace was the porch; justification was the entry door; and all the rooms in the house were facets of our sanctification. Dimensions of sanctification involve God perfecting our attitudes, giving us the power to overcome destructive habits, sensitizing our consciences to social justice and personal holiness. So justification is what God does *for* us, and sanctification is what God does *in* us. By justification the sinner—all who repent—is pardoned and reconciled, received into a restored relationship with God. Sanctification is the growth of Christ within us, making us "holy as God is holy." Salvation, then, is a process—a process that begins with justification but continues as we grow through "perfecting grace" to sanctification.

In his *Systematic Theology,* A. H. Strong shares a striking illustration from O. P. Gifford that provides an illuminating picture. "The steamship whose machinery is broken may be brought into port and made fast to the dock. She is *safe*, but not *sound.* Repairs may last a long time. Christ designs to make us both safe and sound. Justification gives the first—safety; sanctification gives the second—soundness" (Strong, *Systematic Theology*, 869). William Newton Clarke stated this helpful word: "Sanctification is the Christianizing of the Christian" (Clarke, *An Outline of Christian Theology*, 409). Through justification, in our relationship to God through Jesus Christ, we become new persons. Now, through sanctification, the life we live is brought into harmony with our new relationship.

Through the disciplines of spiritual formation, we allow the Holy Spirit to sanctify us, to enable us to consciously appropriate and give expression to the indwelling Christ.

Though sanctification is a matter of grace and, like justification, is appropriated by faith, it does not take place simply "as a matter of course." We must allow the Holy Spirit to work in two ways. First, in a *surgical* way, "cutting off and out of our lives" the residue of the *"old [person]."* We must not act as though once we have received the forgiveness and peace that come with conversion, our salvation is complete. As indicated on Day 4 of this week, pruning must continue. Pride, envy, lust, sloth, self-will—any and all the attributes of the "old [person]," which produce such sins as anger, adultery, covetousness, hate, greed, prejudice, and hoarding, must be cut off as dead branches that prevent health/wholeness and fruitfulness.

In the Second Corinthians passage above, Paul says, "Now the Lord is the Spirit, and where the Spirit of the Lord is, there is freedom." *Freedom* is a positive expression of the *surgical work* of the Spirit. The freedom that comes from the Spirit liberates us from the sinful distortions of our lives, bondage to our "old self" and warped relationships with others. The freedom from sin the Spirit provides is not "independency" but freedom for a new life in relation to God and others.

This brings us to the second way the Spirit works for our sanctification. To stay with the vine/branches metaphor, the Spirit works not just surgically or by pruning, but by *grafting*. As we abide in Christ, the Spirit grafts us as branches into the vine. The Spirit enables us, through increasing faith, to more deliberately and completely appropriate the living Christ. As we grow in that relationship, we progressively conquer the residual sinfulness of our nature, and the fruit of kindness, goodness, faithfulness, gentleness, humility, and self-control begin to grow. As that growth flourishes, we become more Christlike. This is our sanctification—changed from one degree of glory to another.

REFLECTING AND RECORDING

Look closely at your Christian walk, beginning as early as you wish, but plotting some expressions of grace in your life. Under each of the *grace expressions*, make some notes of grace working in your life in that way—maybe with dates, persons, events, circumstances, your life in the church—to get a picture of the working of grace. Enter a starting date for your time line, which will continue until the present.

Prevenient ***Justifying*** ***Sanctifying***

( ) ____ present

Make some notes that you might use if someone asked you, "What do you mean when you say, '*Sanctification is the Christianizing of the Christian*'?"

Spend the balance of your time thinking about how the Holy Spirit works in a *surgical* and a *grafting* way for our sanctification.

DURING THE DAY

Since sin dwells in our wills, we must practice surrendering our wills to God. A good practice is to pray a portion of the Lord's Prayer in this way:

> Hallowed be thy name,
> *not mine,*
>
> Thy kingdom come,
> *not mine,*
>
> Thy will be done,
> *not mine.*

This prayer is printed on page 203. Take it with you and pray it often through each day for the next four or five days.

Remember you are cultivating a disposition of surrender.

DAY 7

BEARING FRUIT

> [Jesus said,] "I am the true vine, and my Father is the vine-grower. He removes every branch in me that bears no fruit. Every branch that bears fruit he prunes to make it bear more fruit. You have already been cleansed by the word that I have spoken to you. Abide in me as I abide in you. Just as the branch cannot bear fruit by itself unless it abides in the vine, neither can you unless you abide in me." (John 15:1-4)

Scientists and others have been talking about "nonidentical reproduction." Barbara Glasson, a writer who reflects creatively about the nature of life and our identity as persons, uses the concept of "nonidentical reproduction" to note that the same DNA permits a caterpillar to become a pupa and then a butterfly. At the pupa stage, however, the caterpillar "degenerates into a soup of DNA so that it completely loses its structure and has to hang around believing something good can come of the mess." Glasson then remarks, "A butterfly just isn't a caterpillar with wings on!"

A person abiding in Christ is not just a person who has been "saved by grace" for a home in heaven—"not just a caterpillar with wings on"—but a disciple who is giving herself or himself in holy obedience to the shaping power of the indwelling Christ, who desires to grow us up into his likeness.

As we have been considering this week, abiding in Christ means praying and practicing loving attention to Christ in order that we might obey him and become loving persons just as he is. It means making sin powerless in our lives as we allow God to fill us—being changed from one degree of glory to another, which is our sanctification. A very practical expression of that is *bearing fruit.*

We bear fruit as we learn how to become a branch and gain our sustenance from the vine.

Recently I ran across a sermon by Meister Eckhart that provided a surprising and helpful insight concerning Mary and Martha, the sisters of Jesus' friend Lazarus. You probably know the story. Lazarus became ill and his sisters sent for Jesus, believing that Jesus could heal their brother. By the time Jesus responded to their invitation to come, Lazarus was already dead. Jesus' raising of Lazarus is one of the most well-known miracles in the New Testament.

The story centers around the different responses of Mary and Martha when Jesus arrived. The big surprise of Meister Eckhart's sermon is that he holds up Martha, rather than Mary, as a spiritual example. The traditional interpretation has been that Mary is our example because she sat at Jesus' feet, listening to everything he said, while Martha was in the kitchen, buried in pots and pans. Eckhart's sermon is insightful. Here is a portion of it that describes the two sisters.

> Three things caused Mary to sit at our Lord's feet. The first was that God's goodness had embraced her soul. The second was a great, unspeakable longing; she yearned without knowing what it was she yearned after, and she desired without knowing what she desired! The third was the sweet consolation and bliss that she derived from the eternal words that came from Christ's mouth.
>
> Three things also caused Martha to run about and serve her dear Christ. The first was maturity of age and a depth of being, which was thoroughly trained to the most external matters. For this reason, she believed that no one was so well suited for activity as herself. The second was a wise prudence that knew how to achieve external acts to the highest degree that love demands. The third was the high dignity of her guest.

> The masters of the spiritual life say that God is ready for every person's spiritual and physical satisfaction to the utmost degree that that person desires. (*Spiritual Classics*, Richard J. Foster and Emilie Griffin, ed., 206)

From that introductory word, Meister Eckhart moves to affirm both Mary and Martha in their perspectives toward Jesus, but unlike most interpreters, he affirms Martha more, saying that Martha is mature and Mary is immature. He even makes the claim that Mary would have to become like Martha before she could become the mature Mary, for "when she sat at our Lord's feet, she was not yet the true Mary."

We don't want to argue with Eckhart but learn from him that service and spirituality go hand in hand; the active and the contemplative life are not to be separated. Staying with our primary metaphor, dwelling in the vine and bearing fruit cannot be separated. Jesus made it clear. We must go on abiding in him—that is essential. But to be satisfied merely with abiding in him without bearing fruit brings death. Unfruitful branches are cut off and cast into the fire.

The object of the union of the vine and the branches is clear—to bear fruit. Jesus, the Vine, came to love persons, to seek them, and to save them—to establish relationship and communities that reflect the nature of the kingdom. You and I, as branches, are to continue that work—that is the fruit we are to bear.

REFLECTING AND RECORDING

Read again the quote from Meister Eckhart's sermon about Mary and Martha.

Eckhart named three things that caused Mary to sit at Jesus' feet, and three things that caused Martha to run about and serve him. He makes the point that both are worthy expressions, but that Martha has found the way of expressing her love and commitment through service. Look at your own life in light of these two persons. Are you a Mary or a Martha? Have you been made to feel guilty because you are too much like Martha, not giving enough time to "sitting at Jesus' feet"? Conversely, do you sometimes feel guilty because you are spending too much time "loving Jesus" and not enough time "loving your neighbor"?

Prayer is not an escape from reality; it is practical. Abiding in Christ as living prayer, we struggle with being in the world as those who love as Jesus loved. This loving as Jesus loved produces the fruit Jesus says we will bear if we abide in him.

Name two of the most transparently Christian persons you know:

Make some notes about the fruit you see them bearing.

Are these persons more like Mary or Martha? How do they reflect a deep devotion to Christ and yearning for fellowship with him as well as a reaching out in love to the world?

DURING THE DAY

Continue surrendering your will through your use of the Lord's Prayer, and don't forget you are cultivating a disposition of surrender.

GROUP MEETING FOR WEEK SEVEN

INTRODUCTION

Last week you may have discussed whether your group wants to continue meeting. Here are possibilities to consider.

1. Select two or three weeks of this workbook that were especially challenging or meaningful. Repeat those weeks in more depth to extend your time together.
2. Decide to continue meeting as a group, using another resource. Ask two or three persons to meet and bring resource suggestions to the group next week. I noted two possibilities last week: *The Workbook of Living Prayer* and *The Workbook on Becoming Alive in Christ.*

If you find this workbook style meaningful, you will note several others listed on the "About the Author" page.

One or two persons may decide to recruit and lead another group through this workbook. Many people are looking for a small-group experience, and this is a way to respond to their need.

SHARING TOGETHER

1. Since you have only one more group meeting for this workbook, invite two or three persons to share what this experience has meant to them thus far.

2. In your reflecting and recording period on Day 1, you were asked to recall an experience when God got your attention and presented himself to you. Invite two or three persons to share those experiences.

3. In Ambassador Laney's testimony, which I shared on Day 2, Jim said, "They now saw us as not one *of* them but one *with* them." Spend a bit of time discussing the difference in relationship.

4. Invite someone to read aloud de Caussade's quote on Day 3 of this week (page 161). Then spend some time discussing the claim that *obedience means abandoning ourselves to God.* How does the acceptance of this fact impact our self-will, our praying, how we see ourselves?

5. Continue discussing obedience and abandonment by responding to this claim: *We have a right to ask, to seek, and to know the will of God, but once we know it, nothing but obedience will do.*

6. On Day 4, you were asked to respond to the statement, *It isn't the "bad" things we do that spell spiritual dryness or even ruin for most of us but the good things that become overly important.* Spend some time talking about the relevance of that to your life. How might the "expulsive power of a new affection" work in your life in relation to some of those "affections" that may be threatening dryness, even ruin?

7. Invite two or three people to share their personal response to this claim: *The greatest barrier to the full expression of the Christian faith and way is the all-too-prevalent notion that we are victims of our human nature, thus not prone to sin, but unable "not to sin."* Are we helpless victims to sin? Do we believe that the indwelling Christ makes sin powerless in controlling us? What is our personal experience with a particular destructive habit, or sinful attitude?

8. Invite one or two persons to share how prevenient, justifying, and sanctifying grace have worked in their lives.

9. Spend a bit of time discussing Eckhart's interpretation of Mary and Martha. Do you agree? What new insights are in this understanding? If you have seen yourself as a Mary or Martha, how does this new characterization impact your self-image?

PRAYING TOGETHER

Close your time together in community prayer. Invite persons to share concerns and needs; then ask volunteers to offer sentence prayers. Close by praying together the prayer you have been praying this week.

LIVING PRAYER

Day 1

CHRIST, THE ONGOING SHAPING POWER OF OUR LIVES

> But thanks be to God, who in Christ always leads us in triumphal procession, and through us spreads in every place the fragrance that comes from knowing him. For we are the aroma of Christ to God among those who are being saved and among those who are perishing; to the one a fragrance from death to death, to the other a fragrance from life to life. Who is sufficient for these things? For we are not peddlers of God's word like so many; but in Christ we speak as persons of sincerity, as persons sent from God and standing in his presence. (2 Corinthians 2:14-17)

I have an idea that you may have discovered that *living* as we use it in connection with prayer (living prayer) may be an adjective or a verb. As an adjective, it describes prayer as a lively, vibrant expression of our lives . . . praying. As a verb, it is active and calls for action; we are to *live* prayer. Hopefully, this last week of our journey will be a challenge to launch you both on the practice of *living* (adjective) prayer and a life *living* (verb) prayer. Abiding in Christ, our praying and our living are inseparable.

We stated early in our workbook journey that one of the most important truths we must claim as Christians is that the presence of God in Jesus Christ is not experienced only on occasion, but the indwelling Christ is to be the shaping power of our lives.

In the above passage, Paul uses the picture of incense to offer a fascinating word about the gospel and the influence of Christians. He refers to the sharing of the gospel as the diffusing of the *"fragrance that comes from knowing him."* We Christians are to be the *"aroma of Christ to God."*

As we have contended from the beginning of this workbook journey, all depends upon our relationship, our right relationship to Christ. That *right* relationship is one of complete faith, entire surrender, and ongoing unbroken relationship with Christ. Again, the presence of God in Jesus Christ is not to be experienced only on occasion, but the indwelling Christ is to become the shaping power of our lives. There is no separation of prayer from the whole of spirituality. Thus our claim: abiding in Christ is the way of living prayer.

A word from the introduction of E. Stanley Jones's *In Christ* states the issue clearly.

> The phrase "in Christ" is the ultimate phrase in the Christian faith, for it locates us in a Person—the Divine Person—and it locates us in Him here and now. It brings us to the

> ultimate relationship—"in." Obviously this "in" brings us nearer than "near Christ," "following Christ," "believing in Christ," or even "committed to Christ." You cannot go further or deeper than "in." (Jones, introduction to *In Christ*, no page number)

Later in his book, Brother Stanley says, "When you are in Christ you come under a new set of laws of life, new attitudes, new culture, new outlook, new spirit. You are a citizen of a new 'country.' You inherit the resources of Christ. Everything that belongs to Him belongs to you" (ibid., 100).

In my *Workbook on Lessons from the Saints*, I shared a story that challenges us in claiming the possibility of the shaping power of the indwelling Christ:

> In 1963, the atomic submarine USS *Thresher* disappeared in the depths of the ocean. . . . Experts surmised that the submarine had gone so deep that it simply went out of control. . . .
>
> Some years later, . . . because of technological advances, another submarine descended. . . . The crew in this little sub discovered the *Thresher*—a strange sight. They found that it had imploded—exploded in on itself. . . . The surprising thing about the whole situation was that around the crushed *Thresher* were all sorts of sea creatures. They had huge eyes and very thin skin, yet they swam around the *Thresher* in the extreme environment of the same pressure that had crushed a steel machine as though it were a toy. How could these sea creatures survive in that pressure? Scientists, writing about the phenomenon, told us that inside these sea creatures was an *opposite and equal* pressure to the pressure outside them. (Dunnam, *Workbook on Lessons from the Saints*, 72)

This is a parable for us—the way we are to live our lives as Christians. Again, pay attention to my working understanding of spiritual formation: that "dynamic process of receiving through faith and appropriating through commitment, discipline, and action, the living Christ into our own life to the end that our life will conform to and manifest the reality of Christ's presence in the world." With this understanding, there is no separation of prayer from the whole of our life. So, as I indicated early in our workbook journey, a big part of our praying "is recognizing, cultivating awareness of, and giving expression to the indwelling Christ." The presence of God in Jesus Christ must not be something we experience only occasionally; rather, the indwelling Christ must become the shaping power of our life.

REFLECTING AND RECORDING

Reflect on the claim that the presence of God in Jesus Christ must not be something we experience only occasionally; rather, the indwelling Christ must be the shaping power of our lives. What are some changes you will need to make in your life to make this possible?

Read again today's beginning scripture and the three paragraphs after it. Spend some time reflecting on what it means for you to be the *aroma of Christ* in your daily life. Then write a prayer making a commitment to be that kind of expression of the gospel.

DURING THE DAY

Søren Kierkegaard reminds us, "Repetition is the daily bread which satisfies with benediction. . . . Repetition is reality, and it is the seriousness of life" (Kierkegaard, *Repetition: An Essay in Experimental Psychology*, 5, 6). As we have sought to practice that on other days, let's do so this week. On page 203 the following statements are printed on an affirmation card:

> The presence of God in Jesus Christ is not to be experienced only occasionally. The indwelling Christ is to become the shaping power of my life.

Cut out the card and carry it with you, keeping it available daily. Repeat these sentences often throughout the day and throughout this week.

DAY 2

NOT WHAT HE DID, BUT WHO HE WAS

> This is my commandment, that you love one another as I have loved you. No one has greater love than this, to lay down one's life for one's friends. You are my friends if you do what I command you. I do not call you servants any longer, because the servant does not know what the master is doing; but I have called you friends, because I have made known to you everything that I have heard from my Father. You did not choose me but I chose you. And I appointed you to go and bear fruit, fruit that will last, so that the Father will give you whatever you ask him in my name. I am giving you these commands so that you may love one another. (John 15:12-17)

Jesus makes it clear our abiding in him results in communion with one another in love. Our mission in the world (bearing fruit) is to express Christ's love in the daily pattern of our life.

He doesn't call us servants but friends, because he has shared with us everything the Father has shared with him. And the "big" thing God has shared with Christ is love.

Brennan Manning is one of the most challenging writers and speakers I know. Part of his power comes in his personal testimony, which reveals his own vulnerability and weakness. I once heard him tell the following story:

> One Christmas Eve I was working with a rescue team in the Bowery of New York City, fishing drunks out of the street. In a grimy doorway the stench of one particular alcoholic was so vile that I asked my partner, an agnostic social worker, if he would handle that one. "No trouble," he answered. Whispering tender words of consolation, he gently lifted the drunk into the van, and began to speak tender words of comfort. I decided to wait awhile before telling my partner about the power of the Holy Spirit in my life, about seeing Christ in the least and the lowliest. (Manning, *The Wisdom of Tenderness*, 77)

Those of us who were not just listening, but had heard him, were convicted. We have been there. As Dallas Willard writes,

> [Jesus] calls us to him to impart himself to us. He does not call us to do what he did, but to be as he was, permeated with love. Then the doing of what he did and said becomes the natural expression of who we are in him. (Dallas Willard, *The Divine Conspiracy*, 183)

Our working understanding of spiritual formation closes with the words "to the end that our life will conform to and manifest the reality of Christ's presence in the world." That manifestation is in word, deed, and sign. And the sign is more often than not in our attitude. How we feel about and relate to others demonstrates the degree of Christ's presence in us.

Malcolm Muggeridge closed his biography of Mother Teresa with these words:

> It will be for posterity to decide whether she is a saint. I only say of her that in a dark time she is a burning and a shining light; in a cruel time, a living embodiment of Christ's gospel of love; in a godless time, the Word dwelling among us, full of grace and truth. (Muggeridge, *Something Beautiful for God*, 146)

After her death, letters were discovered in which Mother Teresa confessed times of doubt, dryness, and desolation of soul. Some critics speculated whether this should change the fact that the Roman Church was working toward canonizing her as a saint. That was never an issue for me, given Jacopone da Todi's definition of saint: "one in whom Christ is felt to live again."

Mother Teresa was one in whom Christ was felt to live again. "Our works are only an expression of our love for Christ," she said. "Our hearts need to be full of love for him and since we have to express that love in action, naturally then the poorest of the poor are the means of expressing our love for God" (Muggeridge, 146).

We cannot separate our life in Christ from the way we relate to others. A spirituality that does not lead to active ministry of compassion and caring becomes an indulgent preoccupation with self. This grieves the Holy Spirit and violates the presence of the indwelling Christ.

REFLECTING AND RECORDING

Jesus "does not call us to do what he did, but to be as he was." How does this word of Dallas Willard challenge you? Do you believe he has it right? Do most Christians think Jesus calls us to do what he did? Has that been your belief?

Spend a few minutes thinking about what changes you would have to make, or what you would have to "add to" your life, if Willard is right.

If we would be as Jesus was, then, says Willard, "the doing of what he did and said becomes the natural expression of who we are in him." Earlier in the workbook we talked about the difference between *being in* Christ and *following* Christ. Think about your own journey—can anyone follow Christ for long without *being in* Christ?

Jacopone da Todi defined a saint as "one in whom Christ is felt to live again." Name someone you know who fits that definition. Describe that person here. How does that person live? What does he or she do? How does this person relate to others? What about the person makes you feel Christ lives in him or her?

What qualities in the person you described as a saint are missing from your life? How might you claim and cultivate at least one of these qualities?

DURING THE DAY

Find a person today with whom to share da Todi's definition of what it means to be a saint. Give your friend a chance to reflect, question, and respond to that definition.

Continue rehearsing the affirmation about the presence of God in Jesus Christ (see Day 1, During the Day).

Day 3

JESUS IN OTHERS

> See what love the Father has given us, that we should be called children of God; and that is what we are. The reason the world does not know us is that it did not know him. Beloved, we are God's children now; what we will be has not yet been revealed. What we do know is this: when he is revealed, we will be like him, for we will see him as he is. And all who have this hope in him purify themselves, just as he is pure. (1 John 3:1-3)

Everyone belongs to a family. John, our scripture writer, wants to make sure that believers claim their place in God's family. Eugene Peterson captures the feeling of excitement and joy about that. "What marvelous love the Father has extended to us! Just look at it—we're called children of God! That's who we really are" (1 John 3:1, The Message).

The Christian life is not only about loving God more fully but also about deepening our awareness of God's great love for us. The two go together—our loving God and claiming the fact that God loves us. The more consistently and deeply we abide in Christ, the more real this two-way love becomes.

One of the themes in the personal life of Jesus is his growing intimacy in trust and love with the Father. This is signaled in his name for God: *Abba*. For this name to come from the carpenter of Nazareth scandalized both the theology and the public opinion of Israel. Twice a day the devout Jew prayed the Shema: "Hear, O Israel: The Lord our God, the Lord is one" (Deut. 6:4, niv). God was the Absolute, the One, the Eternal—removed, and mysterious, "high and lifted up," the 'I Am Who I Am.'"

Abba was the intimate way Jewish children addressed their fathers, the name Jesus used in addressing Joseph. It was like calling God "Daddy" or "Papa." In his ministry Jesus used this intimate term to address God. This is not only unprecedented in Judaism but in all the world's great religions. New Testament scholar Joachim Jeremias says that Jesus' use of the term *Abba* for God "is rooted in the heart of the gospel" (Jeremias, *The Parables of Jesus*, 191).

Jesus invites us to share this intimate and transforming relationship. Paul describes it: "For all who are led by the Spirit of God are children of God. For you did not receive a spirit of slavery to fall back into fear, but you have received a spirit of adoption. When we cry 'Abba! Father!' it is that very Spirit bearing witness with our spirit that we are children of God" (Rom. 8:14-16). I like the way Peterson translates this word of Paul:

> God's Spirit beckons. There are things to do and places to go! This resurrection life you received from God is not a timid, grave-tending life. It's adventurously expectant, greeting God with a childlike "What's next, Papa?" God's Spirit touches our spirits and confirms who we really are. We know who he is, and we know who we are: Father and children. And we know we are going to get what's coming to us—an unbelievable inheritance! (THE MESSAGE)

We need to register two truths. First, our identity is in being *children of God*—God who is Abba. Two, as *Abba's children*, we are family. Because we belong to Abba, we belong to each other. As we abide in Jesus, we learn that the secret of our relationship with Jesus is in the essence of his relationship to the Father. "As the Father has loved me," Jesus said, "so I have loved you" (John 15:9). It follows that as Jesus has loved us, so we love others. The love of God and the love of neighbor are inseparable.

I often begin retreat sessions with these words: "The love of Jesus in me greets the love of Jesus in you and brings us together in the name of the Father, the Son, and the Holy Spirit." It is essential that as we profess Jesus Christ's presence in us, we also recognize his presence in others. This is made scathingly clear in the parable of the Last Judgment, "Truly I tell you, just as you did it to one of the least of these *who are members of my family*, you did it to me" (Matt. 25:40, emphasis added). Christ is in me, and Christ is in you.

In *Alive in Christ*, I wrote:

> My working understanding of prayer and spiritual formation requires the presence of the Incarnation of God in Jesus Christ to become a personal reality in us. Our prayer and our life is in Christ. Being spiritually formed as Christians means being conformed to Christ's life, *so that our lives manifest the reality of his presence in the world.* Prayer and prayerful living is recognizing and cultivating the awareness of Christ's presence and expressing that presence in our relationships in the world. As we grow vividly alive in Christ, his Spirit is expressed through us, and the fantastic and thrilling rubric for our lives becomes a viable possibility: *we will be Christ to, and/or receive Christ from every person we meet.* (*Alive in Christ*, 134)

REFLECTING AND RECORDING

When you think of God, when you pray, or when you talk about God, what names do you use for God? List four or five.

Circle the two names you use most often.

Underline the name you use most often in prayer.

Spend a bit of time thinking about God as Abba. How does the name Abba fit with the names you use most? Is Abba closer to the name you use for God in prayer than the names you use otherwise? Are you comfortable thinking of God as Abba?

Spend the balance of your time thinking about the implications of this truth: As we grow vividly alive in Christ, his Spirit is expressed through us—thus we will be Christ to and/or receive Christ from every person we meet.

DURING THE DAY

Test the possibility today: see how many people you can be Christ to. Be open to receiving Christ from those people as well.

Continue affirming the presence of God in Jesus Christ.

Day 4

A FORGIVING PRESENCE

Then Jesus said, "There was a man who had two sons. The younger of them said to his father, 'Father, give me the share of the property that will belong to me.' So he divided his property between them. A few days later the younger son gathered all he had and traveled to a distant country, and there he squandered his property in dissolute living. When he had spent everything, a severe famine took place throughout that country, and he began to be in need. So he went and hired himself out to one of the citizens of that country, who sent him to his fields to feed the pigs. He would gladly have filled himself with the pods that the pigs were eating; and no one gave him anything. But when he came to himself he said, 'How many of my father's hired hands have bread enough and to spare, but here I am dying of hunger! I will get up and go to my father, and I will say to him, "Father, I have sinned against heaven and before you; I am no longer worthy to be called your son; treat me like one of your hired hands."' So he set off and went to his father. But while he was still far off, his father saw him and was filled with compassion; he ran and put his arms around him and kissed him. Then the son said to him, 'Father, I have sinned against heaven and before you; I am no longer worthy to be called your son.' But the father said to his slaves, 'Quickly, bring out a robe—the best one—and put it on him; put a ring on his finger and sandals on his feet. And get the fatted calf and kill it, and let us eat and celebrate; for this son of mine was dead and is alive again; he was lost and is found!' And they began to celebrate." (Luke 15:11-24)

It was in the news again: "All Five Amish Girls Disabled" (headline in *The Baltimore Sun*, Nov. 16, 2006). One of the five survivors of the horrendous schoolhouse massacre on October 6, 2006, in southeastern Pennsylvania is "fully disabled from a severe head wound and unlikely to recover, and the other four have disabilities that probably will be permanent," according to a doctor familiar with their case.

The survivors' injuries were part of the dreadful fallout of the hostage taking of ten girls in a one-room school by a milk truck driver, Charles Carl Roberts IV, on October 2. The other five girls were killed, shot in the attack, and the thirty-two-year-old gunman committed suicide. The survivors were left to suffer physically and emotionally for the rest of their lives.

One wonders how these young girls will respond and appropriate the beliefs and commitments of their Amish community. The Amish have witnessed powerfully to nonviolence, turning the other cheek, renouncing the sword, returning good for evil, and forgiving one's enemies. The most ardent Christians find it almost impossible to believe that the parents of these girls forgave Roberts for imprisoning their children, murdering some, and maiming the others; even going so far as to forgive him for intending to sexually molest these little ones.

But they forgave him. They did it because they believe this is precisely what Jesus expected them to do. Sure, Roberts may have been driven by demons in the inner darkness of his soul. Sure, the deed was as heinous as could be imagined. Sure, we humans find forgiveness to be tough and demanding in far less painful and hateful experiences than five little girls murdered. But it didn't seem to be a question for discussion in this community. They invited the widow of the man who killed their children to the funerals of their children. They insisted that some of the money raised to help them be used to help her. Some of them even attended the graveside service of the man who had stolen their children from them.

It was a dramatic picture of a core dynamic of the Christian faith. Forgiveness was at the heart of Jesus' teaching and ministry, because he knew that forgiveness is a restorative, healing event. The indwelling Christ is a forgiving presence in our lives. As we abide in him, we become and stay aware of the double need in our lives—the need to be forgiven and the need to forgive others. As a living presence in our lives, Christ continues the ministry he preached and practiced during his earthly life.

There is absolutely no reason for any of us to go to bed any night in turmoil of conscience because we are burning with shame and guilt; no need for us to spend another day broken up inside, lonely, and desolate because we feel separated from God; no reason to feel "lost," away from home with no spiritual dwelling place. We are accepted by God through Jesus Christ. The indwelling Christ is that forgiving presence.

Our main point here is that we are to continue that dynamic work of Christ ourselves. Just as Christ has been and is an ongoing forgiving presence in our lives, so we must be that presence in the lives of others. The Amish community understood this concept clearly.

REFLECTING AND RECORDING

Pictures are powerful. Jesus knew this. So he gave us an unforgettable picture of God. Read again the parable of the prodigal son at the beginning of this session—read it slowly, letting the picture be imprinted upon your mind.

It's a vivid picture. God is a loving father (Abba) who embraces the son in forgiveness, places the family ring on his finger, gives him symbols of love and hospitality—a clean robe and sandals, and celebrates with a party. Spend a few minutes thinking of this image of God, testing it against images of God you have had.

When the prodigal returned home, his father received him as though he had never been away. Can you think of a time when God or some other person responded to you in this fashion? Make enough notes to get in touch with and relive your experience.

Recall a time when you responded to another person in forgiveness that resembles how the father responded to his son. Makes some notes about that experience.

Spend a bit of time examining your relationships. Is there someone from whom you need to ask forgiveness? Is there someone you need to forgive?

DURING THE DAY

If there is a person you need to forgive or ask forgiveness of, spend some time in prayer for the person and the situation. Is today or the next day or two the time to act? If you are guided to act, pray that the Lord will prepare the way. Know that forgiveness may not take place instantly. If you are not guided to act, consider the possibility of sharing with a trusted person your situation, and invite that person to join you in praying for the right time and circumstances for forgiveness to be actualized.

DAY 5

FORGIVENESS AND HEALING

> You were taught to put away your former way of life, your old self, corrupt and deluded by its lusts, and to be renewed in the spirit of your minds, and to clothe yourselves with the new self, created according to the likeness of God in true righteousness and holiness.
>
> So then, putting away falsehood, let all of us speak the truth to our neighbors, for we are members of one another. Be angry but do not sin; do not let the sun go down on your anger, and do not make room for the devil. (Ephesians 4:22-32)

In this passage the writer provides a sharp contrast between the "old" life and the "new." Sin numbs the conscience and makes one insensitive to the pain and guilt that result from sin. Since these Ephesian Christians are no longer captive to sin, they must forsake their former lifestyle and behavior and live like the new persons in Christ they have become. "Put away your former way of life, your old self . . . clothe yourselves with the new self according to the likeness of God . . . be angry but do not sin; . . . do not let the sun go down on your anger." Then there is the very forthright instruction "Put away from you all bitterness and wrath and anger and wrangling and slander, together with all malice, and be kind to one another, tender-hearted, forgiving one another, as God in Christ has forgiven you" (vv. 31-32).

Wow—forgive as God has forgiven you! God's forgiveness is *costly*. Jesus paid the high price of the cross. God's forgiveness is *generous*; the Almighty forgives with no conditions attached. Forgiven, we stand before God as though we had never sinned.

How desperately we need the indwelling presence of Christ, not only to be that forgiving presence for us but also to remind us and empower us to be that forgiving presence for others.

Yesterday we recalled the dramatic picture of forgiveness by the Amish community. Ten days after the schoolhouse shootings, the newspaper carried a picture of the little one-room schoolhouse and another of a backhoe destroying the painful symbol of the massacre of those five innocent girls. The bloodstained building would be no more. The news of this event, reported from Nickel Mines, Pennsylvania, stated, "Only a bare patch of earth was left behind, and it was planted with grass seed, so that eventually even the footprint of the one-room schoolhouse will be gone, too" (Martha Raffaele, "Site of Amish Schoolhouse Shooting Razed," *Washington Post*, October 12, 2006).

It was an effort to put an end to the awful event, to wipe the slate clean. But what about the memory, especially for the five surviving girls? We hear it all the time: "I forgive, but I will never forget." But doesn't forgiveness mean forgetting—at least to some degree—forgetting to the point that the residual memory of the issues, the events, the relationships involved does not dominate our response to life as it comes to us?

The indwelling Christ is not only a forgiving presence but a healing one. Forgiving and healing go together—especially the healing of memory. Paul was far ahead of his time in terms of modern psychology and mental/emotional health when he admonished, "Do not let the sun go down on your anger." You've probably heard the saying "We don't keep secrets; our secrets keep us." Bitterness, anger, and grudges, harbored within, either become disease or give disease an easier path into our life. The fact is, forgiveness has not been fully appropriated—forgiveness has not yet worked its healing power—as long as memory continues to dominate.

In his hymn "O for a Thousand Tongues to Sing," Charles Wesley makes the uplifting claim, "He breaks the power of canceled sin, he sets the prisoner free." Too many of us carry the burden of canceled sin. Though we know forgiveness, our memories have not been healed. We carry around a burden inside that no one knows about. But, like a malignancy, it grows and spreads its poison through us. Canceled sin can still exert destructive power.

How, then, do we break the power of canceled sin? How do we cast this burden aside? A key comes in confession and inner healing. I believe that usually not only confession to God but also to another is essential for healing release from the power of canceled sin. Honestly opening our lives in confession allows the poisonous guilt to flow out. Confession becomes the cleansing process that frees the self.

The two requisites for redemptive confession are these: (1) trust in the person or group to whom you confess, and (2) confession that is not destructive of another. We dare not disregard the health and wholeness of another in order to seek our own release. If we abide in Christ and willingly receive Christ from others, healing can come, following forgiveness, when the burden of canceled sin is lifted through confession.

Interestingly, the Amish destroyed the bloodstained schoolhouse in which their children had died before daybreak. But what they really did—forgiving the man who killed their daughters—was a daylight, daybreaking, night-shattering act. And they did it because that's what Christ does. He forgives.

When any one of us is tempted to say forgiveness is impossible or that kingdom living is unreal, remember we have seen it done. The Amish in Nickel Mines, Pennsylvania, have shown us the way. Cultivating the presence of the indwelling Christ makes such forgiving possible for us.

REFLECTING AND RECORDING

Begin your reflection by centering on the *costly* and *generous* forgiveness of God. Get a picture of the cross in your mind—Jesus' death. Live with that image for a few minutes.

Now live with the fact that Jesus' death was for you—with no strings attached, a *generous* forgiveness for the receiving.

Spend a few minutes thinking about the meaning of this statement: *We don't keep secrets; our secrets keep us.*

The destruction of the Amish schoolhouse where dreadful horror had taken place was an effort to leave the past behind, to cleanse and blot out any sign or memory of the painful ordeal. Forgiveness and healing are connected, and complete forgiveness and healing can't be ours as long as memory continues to dominate. Make some notes here about secrets you are keeping—painful memories that need to be healed by the indwelling Christ.

DURING THE DAY

As you move through these next few days, seek to find ways to relate, acts to perform, and responses to make that will show people that God really does exist.

DAY 6

SERVANTS OF THE SERVANT WHO IS LORD

Let the same mind be in you that was in Christ Jesus,
who, though he was in the form of God,
  did not regard equality with God
  as something to be exploited,
but emptied himself,
  taking the form of a slave,
  being born in human likeness.
And being found in human form,
  he humbled himself
  and became obedient to the point of death—
  even death on a cross.
Therefore God also highly exalted him
  and gave him the name
  that is above every name,
so that at the name of Jesus
  every knee should bend,
  in heaven and on earth and under the earth,
and every tongue should confess
  that Jesus Christ is Lord,
  to the glory of God the Father. (Philippians 2:5-11)

As you read the New Testament, it becomes clear that *compassion* and *serving* were the distinctive qualities of Jesus' ministry style. Paul paints an illuminating picture. Jesus, "though he was in the form of God, did not regard equality with God as something to be exploited [grasped], but emptied himself, taking the form of a slave, . . . he humbled himself and became obedient to the point of death."

Not only is this a vivid description of Jesus; it is also a call to us. "Let the same mind be in you that was in Christ Jesus." John Wesley reminds us that the "mind" of Christ "is both the gift of God's Spirit in justification and the life of love for God and neighbor that the Spirit produces through sanctification. In taking the form of a slave to serve others' interests rather than his own, Christ 'emptied himself of all but love'" (*Wesley Study Bible*, 1441). This has been the stream of meaning in this workbook journey. We paid special attention to it in Week 6 when we focused on an intercessory life.

The mind that was in Christ Jesus, which led to the ultimate obedience of the Cross, can be ours only through abiding in Christ. Our rigid mind-sets need the softening of Christ's mind. Our self-seeking mind-sets need the self-giving of Christ's mind. Our confident, self-willed mind-sets need the humility of Christ's mind. Abiding in Christ, we empty ourselves, as Jesus did, of "all but love."

Jesus made it clear that he calls us to live as he lived. "The disciple is not superior to his teacher, nor the slave to his master" (Matt. 10:24, JB). "Anyone who wants to be great among you must be your servant, . . . just as the Son of Man came not to be served but to serve" (Matt. 20:26-28, JB). The secret of life—life in Christ—is here: "Anyone who finds his life will lose it; anyone who loses his life for my sake will find it" (Matt. 10:39, JB).

The problem is that not many of us want to be servants. Add to that this fact:

> There is a vast difference between the way most of us serve and Jesus' call to be a servant. The way most of us serve keeps us in control. We choose whom, when, where, and how we will serve. We stay in charge. Jesus is calling for something else. He is calling us to be servants. When we make this choice, we give up the right to be in charge. The amazing thing is that when we make this choice we experience great freedom. We become available and vulnerable, and we lose our fear of being stepped on, or manipulated, or taken advantage of. Are not these our basic fears? We do not want to be in a position of weakness. (Dunnam, *Alive in Christ*, 150)

To trust Christ, to entrust our lives to him, is to be obedient. It takes us too long to learn that the degree of obedience Jesus calls for is abandonment. (Recall the discussion of abandoning ourselves to God from Week 7, Day 3.) Paul understood that. The extravagance of his obedience is almost shocking. Look at the following paraphrase of Philippians 2:17: "If my lifeblood is, so to speak, to be poured out over your faith which I am offering up to God as a sacrifice—that is, if I am to die for you—even then I will be glad, and will share my joy with each of you" (TLB). That is radical abandonment, and it challenges us.

My biggest problem, not only as it relates to how I express my obedience to Christ, but in my basic approach to life, is an unwillingness to give up control. Can you identify with that?

Most of us keep a tight grip on the controls of our lives. To abandon myself in faith to Christ is hard even to talk about, much less to do. When I am completely honest with myself, I confess, I can't believe my life is going to be good unless I control it—unless I make the plans, dream the dreams, and then work for the fulfillment of those dreams. I don't believe I'm alone in this way of thinking. And I believe that's the great source of our human misery. Only through trusting Christ can we come to a point of abandonment, a willingness to pour out our lives, believing that we don't need to—nor can we—control the future. The future belongs to God.

Everything we have considered during this workbook journey confirms Jesus' promise "Abide in me and I will abide in you." The challenge is irrefutable: *We can't with integrity acknowledge Christ living within us and ignore him in those around us.* Brennan Manning tells a story that pierces our hearts with this truth.

> In the winter of 1947, Abbé Pierre, known as the modern apostle of mercy to the poor in Paris, found a young family almost frozen to death on the streets. He scooped them up and brought them back to his own poor dwelling, already crowded with vagrants. Where could he house them? After some thought, he went to the chapel, removed the Blessed Sacrament, and placed it upstairs in a cold, unheated attic. Then he installed the family in the chapel to sleep for the night. When his Dominican confreres expressed shock at such irreverence to the Blessed Sacrament, Abbé Pierre replied, "Jesus Christ isn't cold in the Eucharist, but he is cold in the body of a little child." (Manning, *The Wisdom of Tenderness*, 66)

Jesus said, "Not everyone who says to me, 'Lord, Lord,' will enter the kingdom of heaven, but only the one who does the will of my Father in heaven" (Matt. 7:21). Jesus didn't spend much time in the synagogue compared to his life of compassion and service among the people. It is no stretch to believe that God's will is for us to spend our days in the same fashion—showing compassion and serving others.

REFLECTING AND RECORDING

Read again the above paragraph from *Alive in Christ* that describes the way most of us serve.

How do you respond to this idea? To what degree are you bound by an unwillingness to give up control?

Abiding in Christ, we empty ourselves, as Jesus did, of "all but love." To see how well you are doing with that, reflect and make some notes in response to the following statements.

Our rigid mind-sets need the softening of Christ's mind.

Our self-seeking mind-sets need the self-giving of Christ's mind.

Our confident, self-willed mind-sets need the humility of Christ's mind.

DURING THE DAY

Continue showing that God is alive by your attitudes, responses, and actions, confirming the fact that God's will is for us to spend our days showing compassion and serving.

DAY 7

THE MERGING OF NOW AND ETERNITY

> Yet whatever gains I had, these I have come to regard as loss because of Christ. More than that, I regard everything as loss because of the surpassing value of knowing Christ Jesus my Lord. For his sake I have suffered the loss of all things, and I regard them as rubbish, in order that I may gain Christ and be found in him, not having a righteousness of my own that comes from the law, but one that comes through faith in Christ, the righteousness from God based on faith. I want to know Christ and the power of his resurrection and the sharing of his sufferings by becoming like him in his death, if somehow I may attain the resurrection from the dead. (Philippians 3:7-11)

As we shared yesterday, knowing Christ means being conformed to his self-giving compassion and service. The goal of our Christian walk is to *gain Christ*, to be *found in Christ.*

The dynamic power of the gospel streams from the Resurrection. The central miracle of the New Testament is not Jesus' raising Lazarus from the dead, or calming the stormy sea, or feeding the five thousand, or giving sight to a blind man—none of these, nor all of them put together. The miracle of the gospel is Christ, risen and alive in the world.

So Paul exclaims, "I want to know Christ and the power of his resurrection."

In the power of the Resurrection, *now* and *eternity* are merged. First, in the power of the Resurrection, we live in the confidence and joy of being children of God.

Years ago, when I first began my work leading a prayer ministry of The Upper Room, I came across a little book titled *Prayer Is a Hunger*, by Edward Farrell, a Roman Catholic priest in Detroit. I was attracted to his simplicity in expressing profound truth. So I began to "follow" him, seeking to read everything he wrote. Then I had the opportunity to hear him speak. Later he wrote the story I heard him tell.

His uncle, who lived in Ireland, was about to turn eighty. Farrell decided to take his vacation in Ireland to celebrate his uncle's birthday. The morning of the milestone birthday, he and his uncle got up before dawn to take a walk along the shore and watch the sun rise over Lake Killarney. They didn't speak as they stood together, lost in the glory of the rising sun. Suddenly Farrell's uncle surprised him by skipping along the lakeshore, smiling radiantly. Farrell remarked to him, once he caught up with him, "Uncle Seamus, you look very happy. Do you want to tell me why?"

"Yes, lad, I'm happy," the eighty-year-old man responded. "You see, the Father is very fond of me. Ah, me Father is so very fond of me" (Edward J. Farrell, quoted in Brennan Manning, *The Wisdom of the Heart of Tenderness*, 25–26).

Abiding in Christ, we keep that confidence alive: God loves and cares for us, and we live in the confidence and joy of being children of God.

In the power of the Resurrection, now and eternity are merged because we know that "death has been swallowed up in victory" (1 Cor. 15:54).

Jesus often spoke of eternal life. When the woman at the well questioned him about the living water he had told her about, he said, "Everyone who drinks of this water will be thirsty again, but those who drink of the water that I will give them will never be thirsty. The water that I will give will become in them a spring of water gushing up to eternal life" (John 4:13-14).

When the Jews threatened Jesus for healing on the sabbath and for calling God his own Father, Jesus replied: "Anyone who does not honor the Son does not honor the Father who sent him. Very truly, I tell you, anyone who hears my word and believes him who sent me has eternal life, and does not come under judgment, but has passed from death to life" (John 5:23-24).

When Jesus is alive in our experience, *death is swallowed up in victory*, we know that nothing, not even death, can separate us from Christ's love (see Romans 8:31-39).

There is a small Baptist church in Perry County, Mississippi—the church where I was converted as a teenager. The church stands about three hundred yards up the road from the house where I grew up. Behind the church is a cemetery where I will be buried someday. My mother and father are buried there.

On my mother's tombstone is an inscription. It contains the last words she spoke to my father before she died. We had gathered around her bed in the middle of the night, knowing she would not be with us long. We had shared and prayed together and were seeking to love her through a triumphant crossing. My father was holding her hand. Mother feebly opened her eyes and said in a raspy voice, "I'll see you." So we put that message on her tombstone.

On my father's tombstone is the response he spoke to her that night. He simply said, "I'll be there." His epitaph is a profound expression of the Christian understanding of life and death. It is the confidence that is ours as we abide in Christ. We live in the power of the Resurrection and know that death is swallowed up in victory.

REFLECTING AND RECORDING

Spend some time reflecting on the story of Uncle Seamus. Have you claimed the fact that God is your Abba? Look back over your Christian journey. When did you accept that you are a child of God and that God loves you very much? If you have not experienced that knowledge, try to determine what is blocking that claim. Revisit in your reflection the affirmation we made the first week of our workbook journey: *There is a place in God's heart that only you can fill.*

Spend some time thinking about death—that of others, then your own. Do you believe that as we abide in Christ, death is swallowed up in victory? In Christ, we live in the power of the Resurrection.

If you are in a group, your last weekly meeting will be today. Make some notes about your response to this workbook journey, blessings you have received, helpful teachings, questions, ideas you disagree with, directions you have discerned, truths that have come alive, issues you still want to talk about. Be ready to share with the group.

DURING THE DAY

As you move through the day, think about each person in your group; picture each one in your mind and offer prayers for them, one by one.

GROUP MEETING FOR WEEK EIGHT

INTRODUCTION

Today is the last meeting for this group study. You talked last week about the possibility of continuing to meet. Conclude those plans. Whatever you choose to do, determine the actual time line so that participants can make a clear commitment. Assign some individuals to follow through with the planning and the decisions made.

SHARING TOGETHER

Leader: Save at least fifteen minutes to discuss question 10, and leave adequate time for prayer.

1. There is a sense in which the quote from E. Stanley Jones on Day 1 of this week captures the essence of this workbook journey. Have someone read that quote, and spend some time responding to Jones, especially his last two sentences.
2. Discuss the claim you have been living with this week: "The presence of God in Jesus Christ is not to be experienced only occasionally. The indwelling Christ is to become the shaping power of our lives."
3. Invite several people to take two or three minutes each to describe the person they named as a saint in the Reflecting and Recording time on Day 2.
4. Ask the group to name four or five characteristics of these persons and talk about how they might cultivate these qualities in their own lives.
5. Invite group members who are willing to share the most common names they call God, and which of these names they use when they pray. Is it true that the names we use for God are closer to the designation "Abba" than any other name? What does this say about our praying, our understanding of the nature of God, and our experience of God?
6. Invite one or two people to share their experience of being treated in a way that resembles the waiting father's response to the prodigal son.

7. Now invite one or two to share an experience when they responded to another person in some manner that approaches the way the father responded to the prodigal.
8. Spend a few minutes talking about the claim "We don't keep secrets; our secrets keep us." Talk about this in the context of the connection between forgiveness and healing, and our need for memories to be healed.
9. Have someone read the quote from *Alive in Christ* on Day 6. Spend some time talking about the difference between the way we think about serving and Jesus' call to be a servant.
10. Use the remaining time to reflect on the weeks you have spent together. What has this small-group study meant to individuals in the group—new insights, challenges, commitments? What areas of your life need changes? What issue do you need to work on?

PRAYING TOGETHER

1. Invite each group member (no need to do this in any particular order; give people time) to share a commitment he or she has made and/or a specific prayer request. When that is voiced, have a time of prayer, silent or spoken, for that person. Continue this pattern until each person has been specifically prayed for.
2. Your benediction may be a blessing given by someone in the group, or a shared greeting as persons depart. Greet one another in closing by using this word:

   "____________(John, Mary—calling the person by name), *the love of Jesus in me greets the love of Jesus in you and brings us together in the name of the Father, Son, and Holy Spirit."* Move around the group in this fashion, greeting two or three persons, and receiving that greeting from them.
3. Hold hands and stand in a circle as someone offers a brief closing prayer of thanksgiving for the eight-week experience and petitions for further growth and guidance.

The publisher gratefully acknowledges permission to reprint the following copyrighted material:

Scripture quotations marked (ASV) are taken from the American Standard Version.

Scripture quotations marked (CEV) are taken from the Contemporary English Version © 1991, 1992, 1995 by American Bible Society. Used by permission.

Scripture quotations marked (ERV) are taken from the English Revised Version.

Scripture quotations marked (ESV) are taken from *The Holy Bible, English Standard Version®* (ESV®), copyright © 2001 by Crossway, a publishing ministry of Good News Publishers. Used by permission. All rights reserved.

Scripture quotations marked (GNT) are from the Good News Translation in Today's English Version—Second Edition. Copyright © 1992 by American Bible Society. Used by permission.

Scripture quotations marked (ISV) are taken from the Holy Bible: International Standard Version®. Copyright © 1996–2008 by The ISV Foundation. ALL RIGHTS RESERVED INTERNATIONALLY. Used by permission.

Scripture quotations marked (JB) are taken from THE JERUSALEM BIBLE, copyright © 1966 by Darton, Longman & Todd, Ltd. and Doubleday, a division of Random House, Inc. Reprinted by permission.

Scripture quotations marked (KJV) are taken from the King James Version.

Scripture quotations marked (THE MESSAGE) are taken from *The Message*. Copyright © 1993, 1994, 1995, 1996, 2000, 2001, 2002. Used by permission of NavPress Publishing Group. All rights reserved.

Scripture quotations marked (NASB) are taken from the *New American Standard Bible®*, Copyright © 1960, 1962, 1963, 1968, 1971, 1972, 1973, 1975, 1977, 1995 by The Lockman Foundation. Used by permission. (www.Lockman.org)

Scripture quotations marked (NEB) are taken from *The New English Bible* © 1989 by Oxford University Press and Cambridge University Press. Reprinted by permission.

Scripture quotations marked (NIV) are taken from the HOLY BIBLE, NEW INTERNATIONAL VERSION®. Copyright © 1973, 1978, 1984 by International Bible Society. Used by permission of Zondervan. All rights reserved.

Scripture quotations marked (NKJV) are taken from the New King James Version®. Copyright © 1982 by Thomas Nelson, Inc. Used by permission. All rights reserved.

BIBLIOGRAPHY

A Year with the Saints: Twelve Christian Virtues in the Lives and Writings of the Saints (Rockford, IL: TAN Books, 1988).

Bailey, Ann Rauvola. *Personal Prayers: A Home Study for Busy Disciples*. Missoula, MT: St. Paul Lutheran Church, n.d. (www.stpaulmissoula.org/prayerinsert.pdf)

Barclay, William. *The Letters to the Galatians and Ephesians*. Louisville, KY: Westminster John Knox Press, 2002.

Beasley-Topliffe, ed. *Encounter with God's Love: Selected Writings of Julian of Norwich*. Nashville, TN: Upper Room Books, 1998.

Chotka, David. Power Praying: *Hearing Jesus' Spirit by Praying Jesus' Prayer.* Terre Haute, IN: Prayer Shop Publishing, 2009.

Clarke, William Newton. *An Outline of Christian Theology*. New York: Charles Scribner's Sons, 1898.

Dunnam, Maxie D. *Alive in Christ: The Dynamic Process of Spiritual Formation*. Nashville, TN: Abingdon Press, 1982.

____. *The Workbook on Lessons from the Saints*. Nashville, TN: Upper Room Books, 2002.

____. *The Workbook on Spiritual Disciplines*. Nashville, TN: Upper Room, 1984.

____, and John David Walt, Jr. *Praying the Story: Pastoral Prayers from the Psalms*. Nashville, TN: Abingdon Press, 2005.

Dunne, John. *Reasons of the Heart: A Journey into Solitude and Back Again into the Human Circle*. New York: Macmillan Publishing, 1978.

Farrell, Edward. *The Father Is Very Fond of Me: Experiences in the Love of God*. Denville, NJ: Dimension Books, 1978.

Foster, Richard J. *Celebration of Discipline: The Path to Spiritual Growth*, 3rd ed. San Francisco: HarperSanFrancisco, 1998.

____, and Emilie Griffin, eds. *Spiritual Classics: Selected Readings for Individuals and Groups on the Twelve Spiritual Disciplines*. New York: HarperCollins, 2000.

____, and James Bryan Smith, eds. *Devotional Classics*. New York: HarperOne, 2005.

Frost, Michael, and Alan Hirsch. *The Shaping of Things to Come: Innovation and Mission for the 21st-Century Church*. Peabody, MA: Hendrickson Publishers, 2003.

Hammarskjöld, Dag. *Markings*. Translated by Leif Sjöberg and W. H. Auden. New York: Ballentine Books, 1983.

Hartley, Fred A., III. *Prayer on Fire: What Happens When the Holy Spirit Ignites Your Prayers*. Colorado Springs: NavPress, 2006.

Huggett, Joyce. *Learning the Language of Prayer*. New York: Crossroad Publishing, 1997.

Jeremias, Joachim. *The Parables of Jesus*, 2nd revised ed. New York: Charles Scribner's Sons, 1972.

Jones, E. Stanley. *In Christ.* Nashville, TN: Festival Books/Abingdon Press, 1980.
Kent, Carol. *When I Lay My Isaac Down: Unshakable Faith in Unthinkable Circumstances.* Colorado Springs: NavPress, 2004.
Kierkegaard, Søren. *Repetition: An Essay in Experimental Psychology.* Translated by Walter Lowrie. Princeton, NJ: Princeton University Press, 1946.
King, Martin Luther, Jr. *Strength to Love.* New York: Walker and Company, 1984.
Llewelyn, Robert, ed. *The Joy of the Saints: Spiritual Readings Throughout the Year.* Springfield, IL: Templegate Publishers, 1989.
Manning, Brennan. *The Wisdom of Tenderness: What Happens When God's Fierce Mercy Transforms Our Lives.* San Francisco: HarperSanFrancisco, 2002.
____, with Jim Hancock. *Posers, Fakers, and Wannabes: Unmasking the Real You.* Colorado Springs: NavPress, 2003.
Merton, Thomas. *What Is Contemplation?* Springfield, IL: Templegate Publishers, 1950.
Muggeridge, Malcolm. *Something Beautiful for God: Mother Teresa of Calcutta.* New York: Harper and Row, Publishers, 1971.
Murray, Andrew. *Andrew Murray on Prayer.* New Kensington, PA: Whitaker House, 1998.
Niehbuhr, H. Richard. *The Kingdom of God in America.* New York: Harper and Row, 1959.
Norris, Kathleen. *The Quotidian Mysteries: Laundry, Liturgy and "Women's Work."* New York: Paulist Press, 1998.
Paton, Alan. *Instrument of Thy Peace.* New York: Seabury Press, 1968.
Phillips, L. Edward, and Billy Vaughan, eds. *Courage to Bear Witness: Essays in Honor of Gene L. Davenport.* Eugene, OR: Pickwick Publications/Wipf and Stock Publishers, 2009.
Potok, Chaim. *My Name Is Asher Lev.* New York: Anchor Books, 2003.
Rahner, Karl. *Encounters with Silence.* Translated by James M. Demske. Westminster, MD: Christian Classics/Ave Maria Press, 1989.
Strong, Augustus Hopkins. *Systematic Theology: A Compendium.* Valley Forge, PA: Judson Press, 1907.
Thérèse of Lisieux. *Story of a Soul: The Autobiography of Saint Thérèse of Lisieux.* Translated by John Clarke. Washington, DC: ICS Publications, 1996.
Tozer, A. W. *The Pursuit of God.* Camp Hill, PA: Christian Publications, 1982.
The United Methodist Hymnal. Nashville, TN: The United Methodist Publishing House, 1989.
The Wesley Study Bible: New Revised Standard Version. Nashville, TN: Abingdon Press, 2009.
Willard, Dallas. *The Divine Conspiracy: Rediscovering Our Hidden Life in God.* San Francisco: HarperSanFrancisco, 1997.
____. *Renovation of the Heart: Putting on the Character of Christ.* Colorado Springs: NavPress, 2002.
____. *The Spirit of the Disciplines: Understanding How God Changes Lives.* New York: HarperOne, 1991.

AFFIRMATION CARDS

The presence of God in Jesus Christ is not to be experienced only occasionally. The indwelling Christ is to become the shaping power of my life.

[Week 8, Day 1]

A Prayer to Remember

Hallowed be thy name, *not mine,*
Thy kingdom come, *not mine,*
Thy will be done, *not mine.*

[Week 6, Day 6]

I Surrender All

All to Jesus I surrender; make me, Savior, wholly thine;
let me feel the Holy Spirit, truly know that thou art mine.

. . . .

All to Jesus I surrender; Lord, I give myself to thee;
fill me with thy love and power; let thy blessing fall on me.

—*J. W. Van Deventer, "I Surrender All," in* The United Methodist Hymnal, *no. 354*

[Week 5, Day 1]

Hear me as I pray, O Lord.
Be merciful and answer me!
My heart has heard you say, "Come and talk with me."
And my heart responds, "Lord, I am coming."

(Psalm 27:7-8, NLT)

[Week 4, Day 1]

No condemnation now I dread;
Jesus, and all in him, is mine;
alive in him, my living Head,
and clothed in righteousness divine,
bold I approach th'eternal throne,
and claim the crown, through Christ my own.

—*Charles Wesley, "And Can It Be That I Should Gain," in* The United Methodist Hymnal, *no. 363*

[Week 3, Day 5]

____________________, "the secret is simply this: 'Christ in you! Yes, Christ in you; bringing with him the hope of all the glorious things to come.'"

Colossians 1:27, Phillips*

[Week 3, Day 1]

A Prayer to the Holy Spirit

Breathe on me, Breath of God, fill me with life anew,
that I may love what thou dost love,
and do what thou wouldst do.

Breath on me, Breath of God,
until my heart is pure,
until with thee I will one will,
to do and to endure.

—*Edwin Hatch, "Breathe on Me, Breath of God," in* The United Methodist Hymnal, *no. 420*

[Week 2, Day 5]

An Invitation to Christ

Come, my Light, and illumine my darkness.
Come, my Life, and revive me from death.
Come, my Physician, and heal my wounds.
Come, Flame of divine love, and burn up the thorns of my sins,
kindling my heart with the flame of thy love.
Come, my King, sit upon the throne of my heart and reign there.
For thou alone art my King and my Lord. Amen.

—*Dimitri of Rostov, Russia, 17th century,* The United Methodist Hymnal, *no. 466*

[Week 2, Day 2]

There is a place in God's heart that only I can fill.

[Week 1, Day 1]

ABOUT THE AUTHOR

Maxie Dunnam is president emeritus of Asbury Theological Seminary in Wilmore, Kentucky. He served Asbury as chancellor for four years following his presidency, from 1994 to 2004. Dr. Dunnam came to Asbury after twelve years of ministry at the 6,000-member Christ United Methodist Church in Memphis, Tennessee.

Widely known among Methodists as an evangelist, small-group pioneer, and leader, Dunnam organized and pastored three Methodist churches before coming to The Upper Room as director of Prayer Life and Fellowship. He was world editor of *The Upper Room* daily devotional guide from 1975 to 1982. Under Dunnam's leadership, The Upper Room began its popular program The Walk to Emmaus.

A prolific writer, Dunnam is the author of more than forty books, including *The Workbook of Living Prayer* and many other workbooks. A past president of the World Methodist Council, he now serves on the executive board. He is also a member of the University Senate of The United Methodist Church. In "active retirement," he is the director of Kingdom Catalysts, a ministry that empowers transformational leadership.

Maxie and his wife, Jerry, reside in Memphis and are the parents of three grown children. They have four grandchildren. Maxie continues to travel widely and enjoys art shows and card games in his spare time.